For Zoe —
let me know
what you think!

Larry

Darling,
You
Can't
Do Both

Darling, You Can't Do Both

AND OTHER NOISE TO IGNORE ON YOUR WAY UP

JANET KESTIN & NANCY VONK

Collins

HarperCollins Publishers Ltd
2 Bloor Street East, 20th Floor
Toronto, Ontario, Canada
M4W 1A8

www.harpercollins.ca

Library and Archives Canada Cataloguing in Publication
information is available upon request.

ISBN 978-1-55468-581-3

Printed and bound in the United States
RRD 9 8 7 6 5 4 3 2 1

For Farokh Monajem and Katharine Miller,
the angels on our shoulders from the first to the last.

Contents

Introduction

Our story is a counterintuitive one. We spent our advertising careers breaking rules, challenging the status quo and prodding others to do the same. But rather than punishment, we found reward, with ever-bigger leadership roles. Ironic, considering that we started as two women who had exactly no ambition to be the leaders of anything; we just wanted to do good work, enjoy life with friends and family and have fun along the way. In the advertising business, this is more likely to help you beat a path to "early retirement" than the corner suite. But we found that ignoring the norms of our business put us on the fast track, not the bread line. Much of our success has come not in spite of motherhood but because of it. We're women who had to be pushed through the glass ceiling by others (including men). And we never would have become leaders if we hadn't done it together: two, two, two mints in one.

This isn't to say it was a glass-smooth journey. Over our long career together, our rule-breaking ways landed us in trouble. Often. But we wouldn't have done it any other way. And this career-making strategy started with a bar of soap.

The litmus test

In the early 1990s, as a newly minted creative team, we managed to incur the disdain of the advertising establishment right out of the gate when we shattered some time-honored rules in creating a campaign called "Dove Litmus Test." It proved to be pioneering. Not only did we help sell a stupid amount of soap, but "Litmus" paved the way for Dove's Campaign for Real Beauty, which reached millions of people and sparked a global debate about our culture's warped definition of beauty. For us, it ignited a personal interest in looking much more closely at what women are up against at home and at work.

The tipping point for Dove, and our careers, came when the brand's thirty-five-year-old patent expired. Our new client at Lever, Peter Elwood, was worried that a competitor had a clone in the works. This was the first time in years that Dove's comfy spot at the top of the soap aisle looked shaky. We agreed with him: the bar with "1/4 moisturizing cream" needed a face-lift.

Because we were new to Dove's marketing team, Peter thought

we should understand the product fundamentals. He organized a technical briefing where people in lab coats gave us a crash course on all the unique aspects of the bar we'd grown up with. We learned that Dove isn't a soap, technically. It has a non-soap ingredient developed during World War II to clean the skin of burn victims. Because of that, Dove is pH neutral, one of the fundamental reasons it's easier on skin: "It doesn't strip away skin oils like soaps do. 'Squeaky clean' skin is actually dried out, easily irritated."

"Which soaps?"

"All soaps."

Do you remember those yellow litmus papers from high school science class? Our new friends in the Lever lab told us that if you pressed one up against a wet bar of Dove, it wouldn't change color because Dove is pH neutral, while other soaps would instantly turn the strip dark blue, indicating high alkalinity. They showed us the jolting color change with five or six soaps, including a "baby soap," to demonstrate that they were all about the same when it came to pH. They gave us examples of things that are alkaline, things that are acidic and things that are pH neutral, for context. Their little chemistry lesson was a gripper. This was an unexpected way to see the big difference between Dove and all its competitors, but we had to try it ourselves to really believe it. We swept dozens of soaps off the shelf at a nearby drugstore and took over a boardroom back at the office to do our own pH tests. Those little yellow papers turned ink blue again and again and again. Every single bar had about the same pH as Mr. Clean. No, that didn't mean they'd peel the skin off the user. But that level of alkalinity struck us as rather aggressive. We felt duped by those brands' ads that blathered on about how mild, gentle, natural and pure their product was.

Sitting on overstuffed couches at Janet's house with Persian tea in hand, we generated a carpet of quickly sketched storyboards as we tackled the advertising challenge. In a single morning we decided to pitch a campaign to Peter that would recreate in the minds of TV viewers the exact feeling we had when we did the test. The campaign we produced was literally a litmus test. Unlike any Dove ad before it, "Litmus" didn't show any women, save for a hand. And in another unconventional move, there was no voice commenting on what was happening to lead the viewer, because we wanted this story to be told objectively. Finally, we didn't end with the "pour shot"—the sacred sign-off through decades of Dove commercials, where moisturizer is magically poured into the shape of a bar of Dove. In this context we thought it would seem gimmicky and distracting. The headline in magazine ads asked, "Do you really need the alkalinity of a household cleaner to wash your face?" The reader could write away for free litmus paper so she could test her own brand. She didn't need to take our word for it, she could see for herself and decide how she felt.

The campaign was perceived as an enormous risk by top brass at both Ogilvy & Mather, our agency, and Lever in New York. They were not impressed when they saw what we were doing in

Canada. We were breaking rules that had been carved in stone not only for Dove but for the larger world of advertising. David Ogilvy, the legendary agency founder, had famously created Dove's first ad campaign. Who were we to mess with decades of success?

Ogilvy himself wrote a scolding letter saying "science won't sell." But the consumer didn't see it that way. Dove sales went through the roof and their main competitors' took a nosedive. The campaign reframed Dove and challenged the way other brands were talking to women. It gave them a compelling, intelligent reason to buy a product and didn't condescend to female stereotypes.

"Litmus" was the blueprint for our success. It was about risk taking and authenticity. There was reward for finding inspiration in unconventional places, listening to unconventional voices and speaking the truth.

We've now worked together for over twenty years, thirteen in the chief creative officer's role at Ogilvy Toronto. We've been named "ad women of the year," been handed lifetime achievement awards and won many of the ad industry's most prestigious honors (just go with us here: "ads," "prestigious" and "honors" *can* all belong in the same sentence). We speak at events around the world, and some nice people call us role models. Today we run our own company, Swim, a creative leadership lab. We're authors (*Pick Me*) and longtime career advice columnists ("Ask Jancy") on ihaveanidea.org. We sit on boards. We've made it, by most standards. But along the way, we've struggled with many of the issues commonly faced by women in the workplace: poor self-esteem, missed networking opportunities, gender bias, the chronic guilt and exhaustion of balancing career and kids. It wasn't a straight line upward on a career graph, and the lows were plenty low. We stumbled, fell, stumbled, rose, tripped, flew. In part because we had each other, in part thanks to the faith of others, in part because of real hard work, but mostly because we didn't know what we didn't know: we were unconsciously breaking The Rules all the time.

Redefining the game

As two of the very few female leaders in a notoriously sexist industry, we've got perspective on what's in your way, and we think it will serve you no matter what field you're in. There are many excellent books, countless articles and other tools out there, designed to make a difference. (We had classics like *Games Mother Never Taught You* on our bookshelves even as students in the 1970s.) But we wanted to try to address some big gaps we see in the dialogue about gender in the workplace, and in the comprehension of what's really at play today. There's still much more to talk about. We know "enlightenment" alone isn't enough; we want to share ideas that will help you build a new plan.

If most women can't have it all, we can have it a whole bunch, to quote Shelly Lazarus, chairman emeritus of Ogilvy & Mather. And we believe that a big step in the right direction is putting a blowtorch to outdated rules that don't serve us. It's time to think a little differently. What if you ignored office politics, took a solemn vow of authenticity and spoke your truth no matter how painful the short-term consequences? What if you asked your boss for what you need to succeed, even as you head out on maternity leave? What if you prioritized mentoring others, even, by all appearances, over your own personal advancement? What if the best people right out of school, packed with ideas and naïveté, could collaborate with the most seasoned for the perfect combustion of creativity to solve problems? And what if, once the leader, you created a culture of teamwork instead of fostering the typical model of "be the hero"? For us, doing these things translated to long-term success.

We had to stop our self-sabotaging behaviors—rules of our own making—that tripped us up as surely as any external force. Ever find yourself cleaning up after a client meeting, playing out the woman-as-caretaker role, while your male counterparts snag a few extra minutes networking in the lobby? Maybe you hold back from expressing a strong opinion because you're worried that people will think you're too aggressive; after all, nice girls don't get in your face. Or maybe you're run ragged, not firing on all cylinders at the job because you do the lion's share of the housework and child care—even if your partner offers to do more.

Maybe, like the younger version of Nancy, you don't think gender bias is an issue in your career. Maybe you feel that if you put your head down and work really hard, you'll get the life and career you dream of. We've been there, done that, and here's the T-shirt: Hard

Work Isn't Enough. There are other forces at play in the working world, and women need to get a better handle on them if we have any hope of creating careers and lives that truly fulfill us.

Advertising isn't just about coming up with the Big Idea. It's about first taking the time to truly understand the target of the brands you're working for. In our case, that target was usually women. We've spent decades studying women's experiences and often maddening challenges. And we've had the opportunity to coach and mentor scores of women through many of those challenges. Here's what we know: there are a lot of women who could use a better understanding of workplace issues—the ones that make them frustrated, angry, confused, paralyzed. That takes a clear-eyed look at a very big factor: those XX chromosomes you were born with. For better and worse, gender is playing a part in the career of every woman at every level. Yes, still. Sometimes it's *not just you*—it's your gender at play when things go badly. And until you're aware of that, you're flying blind.

Seeing and understanding the gender bias that may be invisible to you right now is empowering. We want to help you see what's really going on around you, and what you may be doing yourself that's putting potholes in the road. If you know where the land mines are, you can act accordingly.

You'll hear a lot about our hope for more women in high places, but we don't have an agenda for you to "get to the top." *Darling, You Can't Do Both* is for every woman who'd like more career happiness, whatever her mission. "More" supposes you're not currently bounding out of bed every morning, pointed straight at your goals with blue sky, rainbows and unicorns marking the clear path to achieving them.

We still have work to do

Long after we joined the workforce in the 1980s, so many women continue to have a drastically different experience than men. It wasn't "job done" by the feminists of our youth. We're all in their debt, but they passed the baton with much left to do. Business was created by men for men a zillion years ago, and women have been in the workplace doing "men's jobs" for less than seven decades. Maybe it's to be expected that big problems linger, still directly in your way.

Think of it this way: business is just not designed for female success, despite the unique strengths we bring to the party. The workplace model hasn't changed to suit us; we're still square pegs in round holes. Nothing underscores that like the stats: women hold only about 4 percent of the world's top jobs—and that number hasn't budged since Don Draper's day.

The business world has its own set of rules, some explicit, others invisible. These rules tell women how they should act and what they shouldn't ask for or expect. These rules have created a norm for female behavior in the workplace and punish those who don't fit the mold. And again and again, the rules suggest to women that when it comes to motherhood and ambition, pick one.

"Motherhood" isn't a word normally associated with success in the business world, but it should be. When we became mothers, our careers really took off. The same skills that make you a good mother can make you better at your job and ideal for leadership roles. But the ongoing reality is that a lot of us step back when we decide to have kids. There's a mass exodus of women from healthy careers at that point—maybe because we get signals from both male and female employers that our value will dim when we return from mat leave, or because we don't anticipate support for our pre-baby goals. Meanwhile, at home, it's still common to find talented women with partners who are unsupportive of their success. This is as likely to hold back your advancement as anything at work.

It can look harder than ever to pull off the two-full-time-jobs thing with unprecedented pressure to be perfect at both. It's easy to spot women struggling to be Super Mom at home and Wonder Woman in the workplace, where on top of new time management demands they're routinely penalized (right along with their not-mom female co-workers) for being too feminine or too masculine and plagued by reluctance to seize the spotlight or accept full credit for their work.

We're here to tell you there's a lot you can do to get past the obstacles and achieve your goals. And how about dialing up those happiness levels? You don't have to follow the old rules. You can bend them, break them, ignore them. This book is the how-to, approached in the spirit of Greek wedding plate-smashing. Done right, there should be some fun to it.

We've spent our careers in advertising, and many of the stories in this book come from our industry. But it's not just for Mad Women. The tools and insights are going to be relevant and useful whether you're a professor, banker, lawyer, teacher, nurse, butcher, baker, candlestick maker. The lessons in *Darling* are grounded in both triumphs and epic fails, our own and others'. You'll hear candid voices from places like medicine, the arts, science, journalism and entertainment. There's the odd helicopter pilot. (Speaking of others, we've changed names and details in some instances, for the sake of confidentiality). To state the obvious: we don't have all the answers. We're still learning every day, and we don't always walk the walk. It's a journey.

Nothing in these pages is ultimate truth. But we can promise you a big platter of food for thought, and we'll help equip you to make more money, advance as far as you want to and enjoy your life.

You'll note two voices as you read: as with everything else we've taken on since we first joined forces at Ogilvy, this book was created by both of us. You won't agree with everything we believe and suggest. Robots singing in harmony isn't what we're going for here. We don't even always agree with each other—how boring would that be?

When you come right down to it, we helped redefine Dove's brand by reminding people it was different and that its difference was its strength. We're going to try like hell to do the same for you.

If you have a life, you're not working hard enough.

I got married right out of university. What I knew about a stove at that point was, "Ouch. Hot." My husband, Farokh, didn't have a job, nor did I. Neither of us knew what we wanted to be when we grew up. With four hundred dollars a month for an apartment, and a diet of Cheerios with a Frosted Flakes chaser, it was time we learned to cook. That way, we could afford to have friends; maybe we couldn't eat out, but they could come to us. We mastered Chicken à la King faster than you can say Chicken à la K—and discovered that we loved cooking: outsmarting the dollars, learning the difference between tsps, tbsps and pinches. We started a weekly waifs-and-strays dinner on Sunday nights. First it was our friends around the table, later family, our son, his friends.

Sunday dinner became my creative escape—MacGyvering a meal for eight out of whatever was in the fridge, giving myself weird challenges like attempting three courses in shades of red. For years, it's been my fortress against the assault of the week, and I keep it walled off. For a long time now, everyone who knows me knows it would take a true code red to get me out on a Sunday evening. Clinging to those few hours is one of the ways I've tried to have a life. Sunday night has been one small boundary with a big No Trespassing sign on it. And that means you, boss. But it didn't start that way.

Our business, like so many others, is not respectful of people's personal lives, and working on the "Lord's Day" is just part of the deal. We've all heard about or had bosses like Jay Chiat, who told his staff at Chiat/Day, "If you don't want to come in on Saturday, don't bother coming in on Sunday." It's no surprise that a study by Professor Kim Weeden, from Cornell University, found that today's employers "often expect undivided attention, loyalty, and time commitments from their employees. In some cases, employees compete over who can put in the most hours."[1] The unspoken rule? If you have a life, you're not working hard enough. Early in my career, I bought that, hook, line and sinker. I gave everything to my work because I told myself I wanted to and secretly thought I had to. It would take years of feeling overworked and underappreciated for me to realize that the best gift I could give my career was to make room for my life.

First comes the love

I began working in advertising the year after I got married, hated my first job, got myself sacked, took a break and started again. The second time around, I fell for it so hard that for a few years I literally (okay, almost literally) didn't leave the office. Our CEO toured around at 8 a.m. and then again at 7 p.m., making sure that we knew our hours were roughly morning, noon and night. I know this, because I was there, watching the sunset from my window, and occasionally the sunrise. That was okay with me, because I loved it with a "disappointed-it's-the-weekend" kind of love. Who needs Sunday night when your work is so much fun?

Because ours is an insanely social business, and I think best when it's quiet, I took to coming in early to make a dent before the circus powered up for the day. This didn't exactly mesh with the hours of my night owl art director. Each night before leaving, he hung a cardboard cutout of himself from the ceiling with a piece of string, sat it in his chair, and that was my partner until he showed up around noon and happily worked till midnight. His hours were nonnegotiable. For me, that meant working from breakfast time to midnight snack on an average day. I barely saw my husband except on Friday nights, when we'd go to dinner at our "local," where I would promptly fall asleep in the booth. If you're asking, "Why didn't you work out a compromise where he came in early some days for you and you stayed late some days for him?" the answer is I'd become a bit addicted to burning the candle at both ends; I was proud to be the girl who couldn't say no. If I was briefed at 6 p.m. and expected to have something ready at 9 a.m., I said sure. If the schedule was cut in half, I said no problem. If I had to give up my vacation, I was "good with it." If I were going to flatter myself, I'd say I was the go-to girl, but the truth is, I'd let myself become a workhorse and everybody knew it.

Then I got pregnant with Devin. It was a hard, exhausting pregnancy. The late nights at the office took their toll—not to mention the bouts of nausea and vomiting. My partner remained stuck like glue to his work schedule, and I kept up with the twelve- to sixteen-hour days until I couldn't do it anymore. It was the end of the partnership. When I got back to work after four and a half months, I knew I needed to change my life if I wanted to see my son before he was old enough to say, "Mommy, I never see you." I tried to work a shorter day, but I didn't know how. Workhorses don't say no. Now, baby or no baby, no one could see me any differently. My go-to-girl persona persisted: "Here's the brief. Can you have something ready for tomorrow morning?"

Then comes the guilt

For the first year of Devin's life, I was hardly home. I picked up where I'd left off before my pregnancy, with early mornings and late, late nights. Even with a new, more reasonable partner, I gave Ogilvy the lion's share of each day. I eked out minimal time for baby, an even smaller slice for Farokh, and a sliver for me, alone. It made for an ugly pie chart. It was soul-destroying then, and it's still painful to think about it now. I was letting everybody down but, brainwashed from the beginning, didn't know how else to work. I knew I needed to do better by Farokh, Devin and myself. How would I get some time back? I was young and it took me a while to figure out that the only way to change my life was to break my addiction. I needed to find a different job where leaving the office while the sun was still up didn't feel like a crime, where little windows of time could slide open, and you could use them however you chose: on baby or a movie or sleuthing out the most "perfect pair of cowboy boots, ever."

Turns out, I wasn't alone. In a recent study of more than three thousand women, half of them said they didn't have enough free time, and almost two-thirds said they felt guilty spending what little time they did have on themselves.[2] Once upon a time, there was a line between work and not work. These days, most of us have taken a pink eraser to that line; we're all always on. Free time? What's that? Between 1998 and 2005, the total proportion of free time available to Canadians dropped by 20 percent.[3] Our bosses expect that we'll be available day and night. Our employees expect the same. And then, there are our families. Wherever we look, women find themselves saying, "Sure, I can do that."

Nancy and I saw it all the time. Our employee Zahra was juggling a big tech project and some exciting new possibilities on her retail account when we dropped in a third pin: the client on our global food business wanted packaging designed for a new product they were launching. Zahra was the top designer on our team and packaging was her secret passion. "I'm on it," she said as her face shone with excitement and you could practically see the ideas bubbling in her head. Her workload was heavy, but the deadlines weren't impossible to manage. Unless you had three young children, a lawyer husband with terrible hours, and a furious devotion to perfection like Zahra's. Each night when I left, at six or seven or eight or ten, Zahra was glued to her screen. I phoned her from home. "Are you gone yet?" She wasn't. I called the next night as the minute hand and the hour hand came together at the top of the clock. Midnight, for God's sake. I said, "Please go home. You'll do a better job in less time if you leave it till the morning." Several days later, I tapped my fingers against her door. Through the window, I could see the dark circles under her eyes as she stared intently at her computer screen. I tapped again. She waved me in. "Were you wearing that yesterday?" I asked her. (When everyone dresses in black all the time, it's hard to tell.)

"Oh—this? No. I went home at two, I think. Look at these." The screen was filled with her explorations of bottles, jars and cartons, in familiar and unfamiliar materials. Some were terrific, but there was a whole lot of "well, that's . . . ordinary."

"When did you come in this morning?" I wanted to know.

"Hmmm, I slept a few hours, gave the kids breakfast and took them to school, so nine-ish, I guess."

Zahra was typical of our moms, whose schedule was work-work-family-wor-fami-rk. They weren't driven by special circumstances. There was no new business pitch or emergency presentation; it was just their commitment and impossible standards. And let's not forget guilt, because guilt is the operating system of most working moms. So, they almost always put themselves last. *Sure, I can put off that hair appointment one more week. So what if I haven't talked to my best friend since May? She understands. Yes, I should book that doctor's appointment, but it's hard to take time off work during the week. Yes, I can come to that meeting at school. Of course, I can get that extra bit of work done sooner.* They're busy every second, yet they have no lives.

Time to give our heads a shake

"No way." I didn't believe Dr. Elaine Chin, chief medical officer of the Executive Health Centre in Toronto, when she told me that male executives are more than twice as likely to get regular checkups as their female counterparts. "The more successful the woman, the worse she looks after herself." I'd always thought women were better about things like doctors and dentists. How often have we heard women say, "My husband would need his arm to be hanging by a thread before he'd go to the doctor"? I was always pressuring my husband to go to the doctor, without thinking about all of my own cancelled doctor's appointments, and before I knew it a year and a half had gone by. Guilty as charged. Dr. Chin said that between always being on for work, running to PTA meetings, driving kids to dance lessons, play dates and birthday parties, women not only don't check in with their dentists and docs, they don't even do what they're told when they do see them. Exercise goes by the wayside. Many drink and eat more, echoing the behavior of the largely male cohort they spend their working hours with. Dr. Chin pointed to the East & Partners study of four hundred CFOs that showed that 43 percent of the women couldn't even remember the last time they'd made it to the doctor.[4]

"Men do better 'schedule,'" she said. "If it's in the book, guys do it." So, startlingly, it wasn't the men who were missing visits to the dentist, time at the gym or hair appointments (men make hair appointments?). They deal with stress by taking care of themselves and it pays off. The Centers for Disease Control and Prevention found that levels of stress-related illness such as heart disease, muscle and bone disorders, depression and burnout are twice as high for women as they are for men.[5] Ask a woman, any woman, why she rescheduled her last checkup and she'll likely tell you she did it because she was too busy. I know from personal experience that when in the thick of work and family commitments, this "busy-ness" means we can't see past the end of our nose. I've come to agree with essayist Tim Kreider's contention that busy-ness is a trap, to some degree self-imposed.[6]

Busy isn't all it's cracked up to be
Everyone and her children are booked all the time, yet the definition of a good mom is ever harder to live up to: the pre-preschool,

the clubs and lessons, the music classes from birth. The days of opening the door and letting the kids run off until dinner are long gone. None of us has time to see friends, to hang out or take a walk, never mind to think or breathe.

We tell our children we want everything for them. We send them to art classes and soccer and circus camps so they'll grow up healthy and well-rounded. Yet we let our own lives get narrower.

Are working mothers worse at setting boundaries than working fathers? For starters, I suggest you ask yourself how often you've heard the term "working father." In their 2007 book, *Through the Labyrinth*, Alice Eagly and Linda Carli make the point that in order to fulfill career and family obligations, women sacrifice significantly more of their leisure time than men do. In fact, they noted, "married men have several hours more leisure per week than married women . . . the equivalent of almost five 40-hour weeks."[7] That's two hundred hours more "me time" for them, two hundred hours more laundry and homework for us. But 2007 was a lifetime ago. Surely things have changed? Hardly, if you buy into headlines like "Forty Years of Feminism—But Women Still Do Most of the Housework"[8] or "Doing Household Chores May Mean Less Sex for Married Men."[9] Yessir. That's the kind of thing that has men running to load the washing machine.

But then you stumble into a little crack of light: the recent Pew Research Center study that shows a surprising coming together of roles between moms and dads. Yes, moms are still doing more unpaid work, and dads more paid work, but the gap is shrinking as more women go out to work and men contribute more on the home front. The 2012 data shows a sharp uptick in men's involvement in household chores from four to ten hours per week, and a corresponding downward trend in women's time doing housework, from thirty-two hours to eighteen.[10] The long-term study has been looking at trends since 1965. Moms still spend a lot more time with their kids than dads do, but the trend is up all around. It seems there are signs that men and women both are doing what they can to make life more manageable.

Is help on its way?

Little by little, we're seeing more men like Trent Burton, creative director of Calgary ad agency Wax, father of two girls and the only guy who ever asked us for paternity leave. He asked for three months and wound up taking two years. No one was more gobsmacked than he to find himself wanting to stay home. "I was terrified to ask for paternity leave even though I knew it was legal. I didn't know if I would pay a price for it—would I come back to feeling downgraded or to feeling as much a member of the team as I did when I left? I've gotta say, it was easier to ask women for the time off than it would've been to ask men."

All the wrongheaded notions around what it's like to stay home with kids jumped the gender divide and landed right on

Trent. Ooh, wasn't he lucky? Living the easy, breezy *vida loca*, as his friends said.

Oh yeah, easy. He said, "I suppose it affected my career. I call it my career 'defect.'" He'd been offered a chance to write TV content in L.A., but it would've meant living in La-La-Land, away from his kids. Instead he chose to be an ad agency creative director in Calgary, so he could take his competitive swimmer daughters to Wednesday and Thursday practices. Trent wears the equivalent of a big "Closed for Business" sign on his back from 3 to 6 p.m. There was only one downside: "Dads don't get invited into the moms' groups. No one ever called me up and said, 'Put on your Lulu-lemons, girlfriend, let's take the kids for a walk. My girls are eleven and thirteen now, and I see a lot more dads starting to do what I did, so they'll have a community that wasn't available to me. It absolutely worked for me. And I'm really happy."

So if it's true that more men are putting more energy into life at home, shouldn't that take some of the pressure off women? Shouldn't we feel incredibly relaxed and all "Aaah, now I can read the hottest book of the summer or fit in that piloxing class. Who wouldn't want to box while they stretch?" If only it worked that way. Many women take the bits of time they scrounge up through either careful time management or home front help and plow it all back into their careers. They're well-conditioned to believe that they don't measure up.

Bumps in the road

Women have excellent reasons to worry that they won't be taken as seriously as men, so they just keep on trying to prove themselves against the backdrop of institutional hypocrisy. When men become fathers, it's all pats on the back, awkward man hugs and reward. They're suddenly seen as more "credible, mature, responsible," as a 2010 study from the Boston College Center for Work & Family makes clear.[11] Guys look more stable when there are kids in the picture—excellent candidates for promotion. And us? Well, we're just not to be trusted—what if we run off all crazy-like and decide to look after them full-time? It reminds me of old black and white movies from the 1930s where someone was always saying, "You can't trust a dame." Having children affects the way people judge our competence and how they think about promoting us.[12]

Executive recruiter Cathy Preston remembers a female client expressing doubts over hiring a talented recruit because she was a woman of "childbearing age"—which meant the company would potentially have a maternity leave on their hands. Professor Emily Wall of the University of Alaska Southeast says that when male professors brought their kids to work, people would go all soft and say what excellent daddies they were. When she did it, they would say, "Couldn't you get a babysitter?" At work, we compete for credibility. At home, we measure ourselves against other moms, including our own. Perfect mom. Perfect employee. Perfect wife.

If you have kids, you have a "life outside" whether you want one or not. For most of us, that means struggling with putting in enough time at home, while working doubly hard in the hopes of not being labeled a slacker. As the Center for Work & Family study tells us, kids help men and hurt us, which may be the reason roughly two-thirds of men in senior positions have children, while only one-third of women do. We need to be seen to be doing everything well, to feel that we're giving 100 percent to our different worlds. Finding a way to feed your own needs? What are the odds? It may not seem permissible, but it is possible.

Taking back the clock

Stephanie, a senior manager at a tech company, told me that she'd had this epiphany: it rests with her to figure out how to have the life she wants. She has two young sons, four and six, a busy husband, and a life that leaves her flattened a lot of the time. "I decided not to come in at nine," she said. "I come in around nine-thirty, unless I have an early meeting. I didn't ask for permission. I realized that if I did, I'd put my boss in the position of having to say no, because then she'd have to do it for everyone. I just squared it with the people affected and quietly changed my schedule. My work gets done. No one has a problem with the quality."

Stephanie said that at first, she felt the need to apologize whenever she came in at nine-thirty. But "Sorry I'm late" just drew attention and made it appear as though she thought herself in the wrong. Now that she's trained herself to just do it, things go smooth as silk.

She packs her kids off to school, lets a quiet cup of coffee feel like a little luxury and gets ready on her own time. Who'd have guessed that giving yourself the gift of half an hour every morning could make an entire life work better? Thirty minutes to sip coffee and get dressed slowly doesn't seem earth shattering, but for this time-starved woman, it was transformative. Stephanie's half-hour in the morning is my Sunday night. And Karen Howe's brewery.

When Karen's brother, Cameron, told her he wanted to start a microbrewery and bring the family on board, what could she say but "Lead me to it." Karen is the creative head of a Toronto ad agency, and also a mom and a marathoner. Her kids were aged two and five. Nope, she wasn't busy enough. Next thing she knew, she was doing advertising, branding, design, sales, trade shows . . . and all for a family business. That marathoning was coming in handy. In their first year, Cameron's Brewing Company won Best New Beer at the World Beer Cup. By rights, the added load should have practically killed her, but for Karen, a change turned out to be as good as a rest. The brewery made her better at her day job. "I had a hobby that taught me how to run a business, gave me a sense of accountability that creatives don't always have, made me a better salesperson and in the end, clients trusted me more because I understood their risks."

She couldn't have done it without help. Her husband, who had the more flexible job, became the class parent, fund-raiser and primary caregiver. And Karen didn't beat herself up about not being all things to all people all the time. "You can lose parts of yourself after you have kids, but why should you?" she said. "You have nothing to offer anyone if you're strung out on stress. Doing something completely different gave me perspective."

Karen took a little pressure off herself at home so she could try being an explorer. Men seem to do this without thinking and without guilt. When Professor Beatrix Dart of the University of Toronto's Rotman School of Management describes the differences in what men look for in a job—satisfying career, terrific pay—as compared to what women look for—satisfaction; fair pay; time for soccer, homework, visiting the grandparents, friends—it seems clear where the struggle lies. As Leah Goldman says in the *Harvard Political Review*, "It is simply not possible to work a highly demanding job, cook dinner every night, and make it to every dance recital and baseball game. The difference is that . . . high-powered men are satisfied with this compromise. They don't mind working late some days and missing a game or two or having to pick up their own dinner on the way home while the babysitter feeds the kids . . . For women that may mean feeling as though they are not seeing their children or working enough, but it is a compromise that has to be made."[13]

After realizing that I was a top contender for "Bad Mother of the Year Idol" only a year into motherhood, I decided to make some changes. I reclaimed my Sunday nights and have never let them go.

The price of perfect

When we can't manage it all, we feel harshly judged, by ourselves and by others. *She could be better at the job. I can't believe she missed her son's school play.* At an event we attended a few years ago, the well-respected woman president of a financial institution introduced a speaker, a writer and professor at an Ivy League university. It was an evening event and most of the attendees were other women in business. The intro went something like this:

COMPANY PRESIDENT. Welcome, everyone. I'm glad you're all here. What a treat you have coming at you over the next hour or so. I know it isn't always easy to do these kinds of things. Making sure that dinner's ready and homework's done so that all he (Dad) has to do is get the food into their mouths and put them to bed. But don't worry, I'm sure they'll be just fine. As I was starting to say, you have an incredible treat in store tonight. Professor S. is the renowned author of blah blah blah. Her research into leadership has cast new light on what it takes to blah blah blah.

PROFESSOR S. Thanks for the kind introduction, but was it really necessary to let everyone know what a good mother you are in this particular context?

The company prez is a very accomplished woman with many exceptional credits on her résumé. Yet in that room of her peers, she played the mom card. Was it a little bit of guilt for being out on a Sunday evening? A moment of "we're all in this together"—with lots of moms in that room? The fear of being found wanting on every side of the ledger can lead us to all kinds of unconscious justification, even to a little wry dad-bashing.

Before we get too carried away with taking it out on Dad, there's ample evidence that even in homes where the guy offers to help out more, we'll decline in favor of doing it "our way," or smile cheerily and redo it after he's gone. This need for perfection eats into the little uncommitted time we have.

Of course, we want things done well. The work of home deserves as much respect as the work of not-home. However, that drive to have it all under control—and therefore less mom guilt—creeps into even the littlest things: the tautness of a hospital corner, dishes facing east rather than west in the dishwasher. We say we want our husbands to take our kids to soccer or a doctor's appointment, but we feel terrible when we let it happen, and so we find ourselves saying, "It's okay. I'll do it." Even when it's clearly the wrong choice.

I will raise my hand here and declare that I am actually not a perfectionist. I believe that some things have to be let go of in favor of other things. For instance, I pretty much abandoned cleaning (hate it!) when my son was little because it ate up so much of the meager time we had together. I couldn't make a tidy house the focus of my weekends. Oh, it got done often enough that we didn't have to pretend we weren't home when the doorbell rang, but that was about it. Pursuit of the "house beautiful" fell right off my to-do list.

When Amy Cross, publisher of Vitamin W, was working out the division of labor with her husband, Patrick, he chose to hire help rather than do the dusting himself—which was just fine with Amy. How Patrick handled his part of the deal was up to him as long as the work got done. It's not always easy to let your partner take control of some of the household stuff, but it might give you the chance to do something that matters more, something that will enrich your life.

Like making room for some hard-to-come-by friend time. When Kristi Karens, director of Media and Agency Partnerships at food company Mondelēz International, invited a few friends to a birthday dinner at her house, we couldn't wait. We hadn't seen her in forever and she had an exciting new job. Kristi's husband was doing a disappearing act with their kids so she could have a girls' night. We were going to meet at their place at 6:30. As I was following the winding roads, a little bit lost, worried I'd be late, a text binged on my phone. "Running late. Can we make it 7?" She was going to be late for her own birthday. At her own house! At 7:10 p.m., the rest of us sitting on the front lawn, Kristi's cab pulled up. Out hopped the host and guest of honor, arms full of food. Inside, she plopped down the groceries and waved a hand around the room. "Don't mind my place," she said. "If I waited till everything was perfect to have people over, I wouldn't have any friends." Well played. Kristi is the worst for appearing to work 24/7. She drives with one hand on the wheel and both eyes on her smartphone, yet she's come to terms with the idea that something's got to give.

As part of Swim, Nancy and I give out a questionnaire that asks, "What does it mean to just be?" Women find this question the hardest to answer. Often they leave it blank. One said that it was a cop-out. If you were just being, you weren't doing, therefore you weren't really living. And the moms are the worst, in perpetual motion.

You've got five extra minutes—now what?

Of course, it's one thing to carve out some free time, and it's another thing entirely to actually fill it with something like, you know, a hobby. A few years back, I was having a Christmas lunch with a group of hobby-challenged women: clients, ad people, researchers and media planners. We made a joint New Year's resolution to start the "Get a Life" club. (Yes, we really called it that.) There were about eight of us. The plan was this: each of us would learn something new and fun that could be taught in one night, like making fudge or playing hacky sack. Then we'd get together with a chewy wine and too much cheese every six weeks or so, and the person whose month it was would teach the others. Not so hard. We assigned ourselves to different months. And we never met. Not even once. No one could find the time. No one would make the time. I'm making a big *L* on my own forehead.

It took me years to come to terms with the fact that I'm not the hobby type. There are things I love, and those are the things I do when a window opens up or I force one open. I'm a voracious reader. I see people typing furiously on airplanes and I think, *Why are they doing that when a good book makes the plane go faster?* And I'll happily give up sleep for a few extra paragraphs.

Travel is my maddest passion, so I've tried to make every business trip mean more than a happy client or a sold idea. My passport is full of foreign stamps thanks to my work in advertising. My family's passports are too. Seeing business travel as just a dreary haul through identical hotel rooms is okay with a lot of people. I hadn't realized that it wasn't okay with me until Devin was two and a half and I was supposed to shoot a campaign in Hong Kong.

It meant I'd be gone for three weeks. Three weeks! On the other side of the world! I'd never left him before. And he was so close to mastering toilet training. The idea of missing that inelegant milestone outweighed the lure of three weeks in a new place. I begged my client, Cathay Pacific, to shoot in Toronto's Chinatown, or Vancouver's. "How different can it be?" I tried to get out of the shoot, unsuccessfully. I was sure that if I left Devin for twenty-one days when he was still so young, I would be crippled with guilt and loss, and my little boy would be irreparably damaged. Despite the fact that my husband worked from home at that time and was the parent making the after-school snacks, I felt sure that if I wasn't there, something would go wrong. Yes, I believed I was that important.

Hong Kong was an eye-opener. I survived the separation. My family survived my absence. Distance breeds objectivity, and I found that instead of chewing over my failures as a mom, I chewed dim sum and roasted duck, swam in the South China Sea on my day off, and learned three words of Cantonese from an old woman in a straw hat at a stall hung with sides of pork. Carefully timed phone calls, given the perfect juxtaposition of Hong Kong night and Toronto day, kept me up on potty progress. Of course, I came back to a happy, toilet-trained child, thanks to a dad who was just as capable as I was.

Here's what I learned: to be grateful. Grateful for a chance to live in a bigger universe, and for a husband who didn't care if I had separation anxiety. Ever after, whenever possible, I built in an extra day or two or three when I traveled for work. Sometimes Farokh joined me, sometimes Devin too. For me, shoehorning in your passion can be worth a missed parent-teacher meeting.

Pick your pond and splash vigorously

Figuring out how to have the life we want is challenging for every one of us. Nancy and I chose to be big fish in a middle-sized pond. It made it possible for us to write a blog and books, and in my case at least, to keep doing the things that were my soul food. We had our chances to jump to larger bodies of water, bigger titles, global jobs, but we didn't take them. Were we compromising? Were we letting women down? We don't think so. We believe our work ended up having an impact on women far beyond the size of the organization we worked in. The fancy title isn't the only thing worth aspiring to, and the corner office isn't the only place where one can have a meaningful voice. I violently disagree with Heleen Mees, Dutch economist, lawyer, columnist and professor, who believes that it's the obligation of educated women to *not* have children, and to point themselves squarely at the top spot, or else nothing will ever change. To be clear, I have no issue with running full-tilt for the mega job; I just don't buy that you have to give up everything else to get it.

Chris Tardio of The Lookinglass, a U.S. coaching and business consultancy, works with accomplished women ranging from high level execs in large corporations to younger entrepreneurs in marketing, technology and entertainment. Chris, a very successful fiftyish entrepreneur in her own right, sees a change between the generations. "The women in corporate life who have ascended to very powerful positions have bought into a certain set of rules and stereotypes around what one had to do to be successful. I bought into it myself. What I'm seeing in younger women is a much more flexible view of success and of how to achieve in the world. I work with them on how to work more strategically, because they want richer lives, not just bigger titles and fatter wallets. We work on what kind of leaders they want to be. If I were in their shoes now, I might have made some different choices."

Only you can decide what you need to have a life. There's no one formula. For some it's the top job alone; for others it includes a family; maybe a satisfying, well-paid career, and the juggling act required to get to kids' soccer games, manage date night and make dinner from time to time. For others, it's a hobby; for still others, just a little peace and quiet.

The good fortune of having a husband who works from home some of the time, like mine did, won't necessarily put a big red "X" through the endless parade of childcare decisions, such as choosing babysitters, nannies or a day care—for five minutes if your kid hates it like Devin did—or co-parenting with friends. We did whatever it took to make our life work. It's time to get off your own back, focus on what you need, on what you want and on what it's going to take to make it happen. What follows are some thoughts as you go about it.

GRAB THE WHEEL WITH BOTH HANDS.

Choose with intent. Only you know what you need to be happy. Is it a little more time in your day, some extra help at home, a class or the chance to do good? Do you need to speed up or slow down? Maybe you don't want to go for the big promotion right now because your kids are still young. If you make that choice, don't beat yourself up when someone behind you gets there first. Remember that you chose it. Little kid–hood passes quickly. Have confidence that if you slow down to be part of it, the mark you've already made and your continued hard work will stand you in good stead. I got out of the rat race when my son was three and stayed out until he was six, contributing pennies to the family coffers with articles for *OWL* magazine and the occasional freelance gig. Yes, our income took a big hit, but it was a brilliant three years. When we worried about family finances, I had to remember that I'd chosen time over money and be good with that. As for my on-hold career? It did just fine, maybe better than fine, because it was during that period that I was hired to do a freelance gig with Nancy, and that changed both our lives.

STRIKE YOUR OWN DEAL.

Does your husband/partner know what you want? Support at home is the key to making everything work. Stop sucking it up and state what you need: a fifty-fifty deal. Poet and professor Emily Wall, along with her architect husband, Corey, have three children under the age of six. Yikes. The system they've worked out might not work for everyone, but it gets Emily exactly what she needs. They wake up at 4 a.m. Yes, 4. (Are you saying, "Not in a million years"? I am.) Emily writes through till 7 a.m. while Corey goes to work. Then she gets the kids up and spends the morning with them. He comes home at lunch and hangs out with them all afternoon while Emily teaches. Evenings, the whole family is together. "People think it's hard," Emily told me. "But it isn't. It's the choice we made and it works for us. I wouldn't be able to write if we hadn't designed our own system." Many of the women she knows have either given up exciting careers to stay home with kids, or have ten-hour day care and feel they're missing out on their children's lives in a big way. The more your mate is willing to share, the better your odds of success at work and the happier you'll be at home. The icing on the cake? More free time to fill with whatever excites you.

LEARN TO LET GO.

If you have a husband who is a great partner at home, let him do the vacuuming his own way. So what if it isn't the way you'd do it? You don't always need to be in control. I love this thought from Lara Vishwanathan, head of business planning for Danone Foods in London, U.K.: "I made a massive concerted effort to accept that there's more than one way to fold laundry. Even if it's not my way, it still fits into the drawer."

LIFE'S A JUGGLING ACT AND SOMETIMES YOU DROP A BALL.

Sometimes, having more of a life means that someone gets less of you. Your kids, friends, husband, partner, won't always be happy, but we can't make everyone happy all the time. Life is messy. No one is perfect. Maybe part of "having it all" is worrying about it a little less.

TREAT YOURSELF LIKE YOUR KIDS.

We expend a lot of energy making sure their lives are multi-dimensional, full of learning, experiences and joy. What if you stopped thinking of time for yourself as a luxury? Maybe it's time to think of it as a need rather than a frill. Take a hard look at what's eating up every last second. Is all of it necessary? Could you choose to come to work a bit later in the morning? Ask your husband to make dinner a few times a week. If you took your kids to one less evening program, how would you spend that time? Maybe it's worth thinking about.

EVERY DAY IS TAKE-YOUR-BOUNDARIES-TO-WORK DAY.

Many of the people we work with through Swim feel as if they never see their families, much less do anything else. One strategy that people have been finding helpful is to block off part of the day just for meetings and leave the rest of it open for the "thinking/doing" work. Simply keeping meetings highly focused and strictly to their allotted time gave one group up to 60 percent of their time back—more time to do a better job, time to get home sooner, time to have a glass of wine with a friend.

I've always loved the part of the mommy lit novel *I Don't Know How She Does It* where the protagonist comes home late from a business trip, having forgotten she was supposed to make something for her son's school bake sale. Momentary panic. Stellar solution. She takes a container of commercial mince pies out of her freezer and hits them with a hammer to make them look less perfect. I was the version who did the baking anyway, until I realized that doing it in the middle of the night meant putting in too much salt and too little flour. Excellence is worth striving for, but perfection isn't all it's cracked up to be.

I've tried, not always successfully, to have the life I want, and that includes a lot of things that don't always fit together with ease. Often I felt guilty. Sometimes I was selfish. At times I was sure I would drown.

I saw a bunch of posters hanging in the window of my local bookstore. They looked like classic Penguin book covers, except supersized: the iconic bands of orange at the top and bottom, and creamy white in the middle with black type. Where the book title would normally be, it said, "Go away. I'm reading." When I'm reading, I might as well be wearing that as a sandwich board. I've let food burn and decisions get made without me. I was otherwise engaged. Sometimes my family was all that mattered; often it was the job that won. Outside of work and family, my list of big loves is short: reading, cooking, friends, travel, Sunday nights. Make your own list, learn to juggle, and give yourself a break.

Gender bias is an issue of the past. Moving on, ladies.

I stumbled into my first job as an art director at a boutique Washington, D.C., ad agency and found—to my surprise and my parents' relief—my niche. In a stroke of pure, starter-job luck, I discovered not only a career that I loved but also a boss who would have a huge impact on how I saw women in the workplace.

Sam Macuga was a pint-sized powerhouse. The creative director of our agency, she was not only my boss but the most influential person in the company. She didn't enter a room; she smashed into it. Everyone shut up and took notes—including the president. The 1980s was the era of shoulder pads and masculine power suits, but Sam exuded a bold femininity and individualism. She was more likely to show up in jeans and a sweater (albeit not one out of the L.L.Bean catalogue—she wore one with blinking red lights in strategic places to the agency Christmas party) than something out of a *Dynasty* episode. She was a great mentor. With her example in front of me, I didn't just think that women were equal in the workplace, I thought we had the upper hand.

I steadily moved up in my career, promotions and raises coming at me pretty much as I would have hoped. I didn't think I was anything special, and "if I can do it, anyone can" became my worldview. I would interpret the occasional workplace horror story from a female friend as an isolated incident, not a trend. If I noticed them at all, I shrugged off claims in the news that it was still a man's world, as far as career advancement was concerned. *Gender shmender.* Hard work, a reasonable amount of talent and dedication—what else did a man or woman need? Because that had been true for me and for women like Sam, I assumed it was true for everyone. Many years into my career, when Janet and I stepped into the top creative jobs at Ogilvy & Mather Toronto, my belief that gender bias was a thing of the past was cemented into place.

Maybe because I had it relatively easy and never consciously felt discriminated against, or possibly because of the lasting impact of Sam's influence, I wore supersized rose-colored glasses at all times, and it would take nothing short of a career nuclear bomb to blow them off. It took a very long time, but I did finally see the truth: gender bias is alive and well and holding women back, right here, right now.

Women don't get beer

Janet got hit with a gender sucker punch early on. As a junior copy-writer in Toronto, she was eager to work on her agency's marquee account, a beer. While she didn't drink the stuff, she had no doubt she could learn what she needed to know to sell it. The job of copy-writers is one of research and imagination. They write about all kinds of things that they've never done. They've never been farm-ers, but they can write about insecticide-impregnated cattle ear tags. They're not music promoters, insurance salesmen, restaurateurs or government officials, yet they can create effective advertising for all of those groups. Janet knew it didn't exactly take a genius IQ to understand beer.

So she approached the account director on the brand and put her hand up. It was a big job and she wanted in on what she knew would be a fantastic experience that would advance her career. He didn't mince words: "You can no more understand beer than I can understand tampons." Janet was angry and insulted. His choice of words made her feel ashamed. She told herself it wasn't a moment to act "girly." After a long pause and a deep breath, she said, "I don't think that's an accurate comparison."

The next day, she went back to see him. And the day after that, to insist she could do the job. He finally agreed to let her join the expe-rienced team of writers and art directors dedicated to the project. In stark contrast to her previous diet of small, low-profile, low-budget projects, the big-budget beer commercial meant anything she could dream up was possible. There could be big-name directors and the possibility of shooting on a faraway beach where sea foam could magically turn into cool beer foam running down the side of a cold glass. There could be fabulous music recorded in L.A. and impossibly gorgeous actors, cast in New York. Janet was a woman obsessed, and after weeks of all-nighters, one of her ideas was singled out for inclusion in the big presentation. She thought she had won the ad lottery.

The morning of the pitch, as she headed nervously toward the conference room, thinking through her presentation for the tenth time, the account director intercepted her. He told her she was not to enter the room. Her work was going in there, but the clients couldn't know a woman had done it: they didn't believe that women could sell beer and he wasn't going to risk the business by introducing young Janet. She was furious, but she knew she had no power to change the call. So she walked back into her women's world of Jell-O pudding and laundry detergent.

Problem? What problem?

Janet told me about her early adventures in beer advertising shortly after we began our decades-long partnership. I sympathized with her, but for some reason, her experience didn't register as the evidence it was of a very big problem—baffling, considering hers wasn't the only such story I had heard. There was one from another friend, who told me she was flown to an important client meeting when she was a young employee new to her company. When she walked into the boardroom, prepared to make her presentation, the senior account director winked at the client and said, "Look what I brought you." Another memorable example was the time a friend was sent on a business trip to Miami, where upon arrival she discovered that her employer had booked just one room for her and a senior male co-worker. Her frantic call home confirmed it wasn't a mistake: "Rooms are so expensive! It will be fine!" she was told. It wasn't fine.

How is it possible that a reasonably high-functioning woman can listen to her friends' stories with "GENDER BIAS" in neon lights and continue to believe it doesn't exist? As it turns out, it's not just how blind I was, it's how blind so many of us are. In the late 1980s, social psychologist Faye Crosby made a surprising discovery that experts say is still playing out today. She found that most women are not only unaware of having experienced gender bias, but they flat-out deny its existence, even when it's been objectively proven in their own lives *and* they see other women experiencing it.[14]

In an essay recently published in the *Harvard Business Review*, researchers say the problem is that gender bias is no longer simply limited to the calculated exclusion of women (e.g., Janet being shut out of the beer presentation). It's become much more subtle, rooted primarily in the ongoing underrepresentation of women in leadership roles, where they're in a strong position to create a culture of acceptance.[15]

Translation: I might have had a Sam Macuga in my life, but researchers say too few other women have that kind of role model, resulting in "second-generation gender bias"—powerful but hard-to-see barriers that affect workplace culture and employee interactions. That might mean behaviors like holding back on anything from an opinion to referencing a parental role. At a recent conference for women entrepreneurs, a senior executive from BlackBerry said that in the male-dominated world of technology, "I try not to say too much." Especially not about home life. She's not about to coo over her kids' cute Halloween costumes around the water cooler because she senses it isn't socially acceptable, and she worries she won't be taken seriously in her role as a leader.

Of course, there's still a bottomless pit of examples where sexism's effect isn't quite so quiet. Journalist and author Anne Kingston interviewed a Toronto hedge fund manager as part of an article on women in the workplace for *The Globe and Mail*.[16] Speaking on condition of anonymity, he told her that mocking women's competence was a normal part of the day for his co-workers. "He knows traders who have checked out the speakers' list for Women of Distinction, an inspirational lecture series featuring prominent women," Kingston wrote. "If a female CEO is named, the traders consider shorting the stock on the assumption that the company is being poorly led. 'Why would any CEO give a speech about their gender?' he asks. 'It takes focus off being a CEO.' Using this Women of Distinction rating system, he boasts that he watched one company plummet from $15 a share to next to nothing."

Learning the hard way

My wake-up call finally came courtesy of a man named Neil French, a bona fide deity in the ad business, and a mentor to Janet and me since the late 1990s, when we first met him in his role as the global creative leader of the Ogilvy network. He was a writer, art director and creative director who created the rarest of things: ads people actually liked. His intelligent, often comedic take on the product's story meant his work garnered every industry award under the sun.

We fancied ourselves friends, after spending a lot of time together at "Cadre" gatherings (his annual event for the creative leaders of the most award-winning offices in the network) and industry events and years as email pen pals. When Janet and I wrote our first book, he accepted our request to contribute an essay. We proudly included his name on the cover.

By 2005, Neil had been promoted to global creative director of our parent company. His exit from the Ogilvy top job was sad for us because it meant we'd see less of him. We were invited to be part of an over-the-top, karaoke-themed farewell party. Janet and I donned blue bob-cut wigs and belted out a rewritten Meat Loaf classic. I'm sure it looked at least as foolish as it sounds. By the end of the evening, I was boohooing. It was the end of an era, and I felt incredibly grateful for his lessons. *Be true to yourself. Kick the status quo in the balls. Shoot higher. Don't take any shit.* I thanked him profusely with a face full of running mascara, seven-dollar hair askew.

Now, some months later, Neil was speaking in Toronto at a special ad industry event. Neil told us it was a good excuse to see us and we looked forward to it. Janet and I helped the organizers to promote it, promising a fun, informative and likely outrageous experience from the most talented, politically incorrect guy we knew.

When the lights came up, we saw that an unfortunate choice had been made by the event planners. Going for a visual pun, they had a French maid wait on him during the interview with two industry leaders. (Neil French . . . *get it?*) A ridiculous spectacle.

The evening was classic Neil: equal parts blistering critique, cutting humor and thoughtful insight. The event concluded with a Q and A period, when a young woman in the audience asked, "Why do you think there aren't more women in the creative director's position?" Neil's quick reply was "Because they're crap." He laughed and said he was just kidding, then allowed for some nervous laughter to subside before saying that women won't commit to what it takes to do the top job, so "why even give them a chance?" He made a gesture of shoving a baby to his chest and said, "They'll just run off and suckle something." He spit out the words, and we saw disgust stamped on his face. Janet and I looked at each other in disbelief. Glancing down the row, we made eye contact with Steve Hayden, the writer of Apple's legendary Super Bowl ad "1984." His expression mirrored ours: *Oh. My. God.* For what seemed like an eternity, Neil continued to rant. The innocent question had triggered an endless list of reasons that leading the advertising creative department was not a job for the gender he described as slacker breeders.

Janet and I felt humiliated, furious, devastated. Our cherished friendship was over, instantly. If we'd felt Neil was sexist all along, we had chosen to write it off as harmless. Saying things like, "Meet the highly accomplished Judee Thaidumrong. She's one of Asia's top award winners, and can you believe it? She's a *woman*," at a Cadre meeting virtually rolled right off us. We had become quite good at turning a blind eye or ear on those occasions. We had agreed that no one is perfect and the world is shades of gray, that we'd take Neil's bad-boy, Neanderthal thing with the good.

Being on the receiving end of what we interpreted as a hate speech made me suddenly, sickeningly aware of the real impact of sexism. There was no room left for me to rationalize.

As we left the theater, many around us were talking about their shock: "Was he kidding?" "Was that some twisted attempt at entertainment?" Steve Hayden told us he was worried about what the clients were thinking—many of them female. Students who talked to us were shaken; some said they wondered if they had chosen the wrong career.

Meanwhile, we were expected at the private party for Neil. Some notion of "should" nudged us to our cars; too many people expected us. We agreed to a fleeting appearance, an early exit. When Neil arrived, I talked with him briefly at the bar. In the only exchange we would have about his performance, I said, "You can imagine I have a big problem with how you spoke about women." He was unfazed and offered no explanation. Neil blew it off, and we drifted to other corners of the room. When Janet and I saw Ignacio Oreamuno, the organizer of the event, his first words were, "He dropped the atom bomb."

The next afternoon, I called Ignacio. I knew he had met Neil for breakfast that morning. I hoped I would hear about some version of regret in the cold light of day, but no. He said Neil not only stood by his words, he added more reasons to his why-women-can't-cut-it list over the eggs and bacon. Ignacio ended the morning-after recap by telling me he had watched the tape of the evening. "Whatever you remember, it's four times worse."

Push-back at a price

It became clear to me pretty quickly that I just couldn't leave Neil's words hanging in the air unchallenged, a toxic cloud. If a woman in my position didn't push back, didn't stand up for her gender, he was right: we were weak. I didn't know what anyone else might do, but I started to write. Janet felt the same about the need for rebuttal. She agreed that the piece should appear on ihaveanidea.org, where the audience had bought their tickets and where we wrote our career advice column. I called Ignacio again. "We think it has to be done. Whatever happens." We were putting him in a tough position. This young man had painstakingly nurtured relationships with Neil and other powerful people in the same circle, and he stood to have his own problems for doing what we asked. But if he was conflicted, he didn't hesitate to agree to post the opinion piece.

In my essay, I asked if Neil, a man of tremendous influence, viewed women as incapable, what message was he sending not only to the women looking to him for guidance but to the men he indoctrinates? And if Neil felt this way, surely he was not alone in his view. He just did us all the favor of saying it out loud, and what incredible bullshit it was. No wonder women were struggling to the top (or even the middle) in creative departments. I concluded that women like me were part of the problem: the ones who looked the other way.

The female creative director who, days before, didn't think gender was an issue was suddenly, dramatically front and center for declaring the opposite. If we thought a few hundred people on an industry site would be the readers, um, we misjudged. Within hours, the Neil story seemed to be everywhere. *The New York Times*, *Time* magazine, *London Evening Standard*, *The Australian*, *The Guardian*, *The Washington Post*—all reported that this was evidence there was a problem in the workplace well beyond the advertising industry. One of the most telling sights afterward was the misogyny on parade within the many thousands of comments under the piece ("Female Like Me"). For all the supportive comments, there were many like this: "What a nasty legacy you leave . . . to crucify a great, honest, creative genius in a bitch vent." When Janet later wrote an article for the website that challenged the view from many that Neil was unfairly treated, another wave of bile followed. ("You pretentious, bourgeois opportunists!") Countless editorials, debates and discussions took place online, on the air, in classrooms and in boardrooms. The pile of negative comments on ihaveanidea.org notwithstanding, most could agree that maybe we actually hadn't come as far as we'd like to think.

While declaring to the press that he had been trying for entertainment and had been misrepresented in super-uptight Toronto, Neil stood by his message that women in advertising aren't up to the big job because they won't commit. He resigned from his post a few weeks later. He would go on to "validate" his statements at the event (which included "women don't make it to the top because they don't deserve to") by tallying the relatively small number of awards won by women in advertising shows. Neil claimed that anyone could see the video of the evening for themselves. We wish that was true. But a search won't turn up the part of the talk that provoked the media firestorm.

Bad advice right out of the gate

Five years later, in the spring of 2011, a young woman came into Ogilvy to see me for a career chat. She was a student in an Ontario advertising program. She told me the story of a male copywriter from a Toronto ad agency invited to speak to students who were choosing a marketing major. During his talk, he advised the female students to avoid copywriting or art direction, as they would find it impossible to succeed in jobs that are so demanding, with immense deadline pressures, once they became mothers. I thought I couldn't have heard her correctly.

"Was he older?"

"No, in his thirties."

"Did your professor give him the hook?"

"Well, no, but he did tell us later that was bad advice."

"Imagine the same advice being given at a lecture to female pre-med students or law students," I said. "Wow, is making ads harder than being a doctor? Would someone like that be taken from the room by their ear?"

She was one of many students in North America who have told me and Janet that sexism is still rampant in our industry —even at some of the very best schools. I thought back to the students who had told me that they wanted to switch careers after Neil's speech, and wondered how many women had changed their goals that day, just as I had around that age when one professor told me that journalism was a horrible career choice. The impact of an authority figure's opinion at that stage is huge—certainly it had been for me decades earlier. In just two minutes, I crossed one of the most interesting career choices I had been considering off my list.

Another young woman shared a tale with me, over many strong, black coffees, of outrageous behavior in a university classroom. Caroline Valenta is a friend and a recent architecture grad from a school in California. In a class one day in early spring, she was among a group of excited young people on the verge of taking their trade into the working world. Most of the students were women.

On this particular day, the professor opted for a provocative dialogue. "Why do you think female architects are less well known than male architects?" he asked. He proceeded to show a video about women in architecture that highlighted their achievements. "I'll let it speak for itself."

When the video was over, the professor looked around the room and asked again, "Why do you suppose female architects aren't as well known as male architects?" Students looked at each other uncomfortably. A few looked at the floor. The odd hand went up. One woman spoke hesitantly: "Because there aren't as many of them?" There was a long silence. The professor answered his own question: "It's because women's skills aren't on par with men's in architecture." When some challenged him, this accomplished architect responded with, "Come on, guys. I can't believe you haven't thought about it."

Caroline told me she didn't think he meant to be harmful. Even if one is generous and accepts he had "good intent"—perhaps he was trying to manage expectations for these women when they went to get jobs (I'm trying here)—it didn't stop Caroline from making the difficult choice to write a letter to the dean, decrying the professor's remarks and challenging the university to take a stand on his diminishing of the majority of the students in the program. Luckily, she spoke up in the right way to the right person. The school opted to replace the professor.

You'd hope—maybe even expect—to hear the youngest reporting in with stories showing that corners have been turned for their generation. Are we there yet? No.

Sisters are doing it to each other

If you do opt to call out gender bias when you see it, be prepared to go it alone. When she was agonizing over whether or not to take action, Caroline didn't get support from her fellow female students. Despite their discomfort with the professor's attitude, many said to her, "Why are you wasting your time on this? Don't you have bigger fish to fry?"

It's depressing to observe how many women who make their way into the most senior positions don't exactly support their own, any more than those female students did in the classroom. It's true that many women's organizations and individuals are putting tremendous effort into women's success. Books like Sheryl Sandberg's *Lean In* are exploding onto shelves. But many women in high places—even some of our favorites—aren't all arms-locked for the ones coming up.

A woman we've long admired and who's a super-talented and powerful leader recently said in the press that she doesn't think there's any problem for women in her field. Sharing a lunch with her shortly after that, knowing that her own history included terrible experiences with sexual harassment, I wondered if she would say she was misquoted. That didn't happen. As our time together wound down, gender did come up. She told me she preferred working with men, that "women complain too much."

A small business owner we've known for many years was a welcome sight one evening at the home of a mutual friend. Janet and I hadn't seen her in a long time, and we found a quiet corner for an overdue catch-up. As we compared notes on the latest challenges in our jobs, she talked about her big frustration with a relatively new employee who had just announced she was pregnant. Apparently, in her interview, the woman had told her future boss that her long-term plans were to start a family a couple of years later. Janet said, "Well, life happens. It's hard to guarantee when Junior could show up. Been there." But our friend continued. She blurted out that she was reluctant to hire women because they made life so difficult when they become mothers. We could have agreed that it's not easy for the employer to manage through a mat leave. But we told her our experience was that when they returned, it was worth the wait. Mothers come back with new skills. They're highly focused, have great time-management and multitasking skills, often have more empathy, and we got another bonus: they were now the typical "target" of our business—moms. Unmoved, she said she'd still rather hire men.

We start strong but fade fast

A lot of women would understandably prefer that people focus on their skill and skip the subject of gender entirely. If they're experiencing gender bias, they may not recognize it as such, thinking a problem is just them. Many are content to look on the bright side, and of course there is one.

It's fantastic that women are surging into schools and the workplace in unprecedented numbers. This can reasonably suggest that the tide has turned, that we've arrived. Many headlines have shifted focus to the challenges boys are struggling with as their numbers are plummeting in professions from veterinary medicine to psychology.

But where are the women in the more senior roles? Reams of statistics show that huge numbers of women, across industries, jump off the up escalator by their mid-thirties. "Second-generation gender bias" plays its part. Anne Kingston says there's never been a high-profile female editor at any of the top publications she's worked at. Decades after Gloria Steinem literally had to create her own magazine, *Ms*, to write hard news and grow, women are still frequently barred from the serious news stories. "The men get the big stories; there's a Victorian demarcation of space. Women get the touchy-feely things. They're ghettoized."

Laurie Brown, a seasoned CBC Radio host, observes this about women she's worked with over the years: "I find women in the TV news and documentary business so often default to managing a career and home life by only moving laterally. They don't see a choice with the signals they get. So they take themselves out of the running for the more ambitious jobs they could clearly excel at. They avoid the travel time required to go out into the field. A combination of feeling excluded, fear they can't manage it all and a lack of confidence to go for it—'I've never done that before; I can't do that'—means they have their heads down doing the crappy jobs. Management exploits that: the women will work hard and 'take one for the team' without complaint while the men keep stretching. The men weren't there to get things done; they were building their careers. They wanted the award-winning opportunities. They seized the openings to advance: 'I don't see myself going for anything less than executive director.'"

Ultimately, Janet and I don't believe women are victims to a male conspiracy; most men are not hell-bent on holding us back. But gender bias is real, and it's coming at you from several directions—yes, even from women.

When I think back, I have to say it was probably Sam Macuga and Neil French who had the strongest influence on my views about gender. It took Sam to show me that a strong woman ruling the roost is as natural and as great as a strong man in the job, and it took Neil to show me one of the real reasons there are so few Sams.

My first foray into the world of gender politics put me in a glaring, global spotlight for a brief moment. If nothing else, the choice to speak up meant that one woman got a clue (me), and an important topic was out in the open and examined in a way it hadn't been in a very long time. I'm not asking you to make speeches, hold up placards, burn your pay stub in protest or personally take on solving this issue once and for all (though hey, that would be nice). It's just important to recognize barriers you may not have thought existed, because when you can see them in front of you, you can get around them.

Mentoring is an act of charity.

Arthur was a young wannabe copywriter with one big problem: he worked in accounting. Every night, he went home for dinner and then hauled himself back to the office to scribble headlines and sketch ideas. Every morning, he ran them up the stairs to the creative department to fly them by various copywriters and art directors.

"He has potential," we all said, as we pitched in to help him build his portfolio. After months of effort, the "book" was finally ready, but getting some time with Mark Hilltout, our boss, was proving a challenge. Enter fate.

Imagine this next bit as if it were the end scene from *Bridget Jones's Diary*. We're in the snow, but there's no Colin Firth or Hugh Grant. It's late evening, already dark. Arthur is standing at a bus stop, stamping his freezing feet, blowing on his hands, portfolio tight under his arm. A cab pulls up to the stoplight. Arthur sees that Mark is inside. He leaps over the snowbank, runs to the cab, starts hammering on the window. Mark recognizes him, so he doesn't urge the cabdriver to flee the madman at the window. He opens the door. Arthur slides in just as the light turns green, and the cab takes off. Breathless, he says, "I've been trying to get you to see—gasp—me. Blah blah blah accounting, blah blah—gasp—blah blah . . . put together a book . . . blah blah job in creative . . . will only—gasp—take five minutes." Long inhale. Mark says, "Have my assistant put you in my calendar for tomorrow." Arthur, over the moon with excitement, flings open the taxi door—thank you, thank you, you won't be sorry—and steps out right into oncoming traffic. Mark grabs him by the collar and holds on till the next stoplight. Mark thinks, "He's gutsy, passionate, a bit of a danger to himself. Definitely worth a shot."

Fast forward three months, to the moment Mark tells me he's going to let Arthur go. "He's smart, but he can't write. A writer has to be able to write." He was right, of course. Arthur was good with an idea and deft with a headline, but when it came to paragraphs and punctuation, he floundered badly.

"I can save him," I blurted out in my best Superman voice. What was I thinking? I'd never taught anyone anything. I was still learning every day myself, but the guy had put his actual life on the line trying to get the job. I couldn't let him go without a fight.

"Okay," Mark told me, "you've got six months. If it doesn't work out, he goes. And so do you." Me? Wait just a minute. Trust me, I'm really not that self-sacrificing. If I'd had any idea that that was how it would go, I wouldn't have been so quick to offer. I wasn't sure I had the chops to mentor anyone, but I'd said I could do it and now I was stuck. "If they're in grade one and you're in grade two, you can be the teacher," my husband said when I complained about the situation I'd created for myself. I had plenty on my plate and my own career to worry about. I worked in advertising, not the Girl Guides of Canada. I didn't need another badge. Tying shoes. Check. Pitching a tent. Check. Offering to help Arthur had just doubled my workload and the only thing in it for me was keeping a job I already had. Talk about incentive. Mentoring. Check.

It seemed to me that mentoring was something that "nice" people did to help others along, borderline charity that I wasn't sure I had the time or skill for. But I knew for sure that I didn't have a choice. What I didn't realize was that mentoring was far from good-deed-doing. It was the groundwork for a different future—for Arthur and for me.

Paying it backward

The concept of mentoring comes from Homer's *Odyssey*, written in the eighth century B.C., so not a new idea. It was the earliest form of hands-on teaching where the experienced masters educated novices into a trade. When you look at the career paths of highly successful people, they're usually littered with formative mentors, as President Obama pointed out in his 2010 speech marking National Mentoring Month.[17] He talked about Maya Angelou, whose teacher challenged her to read every last book in her school's minute library; Steve Jobs, whose grade four teacher urged him to trade mayhem for math; Ray Charles, whose next-door neighbor taught him to play piano at the tender age of three; and Dr. Elizabeth Blackburn, who inspired her protégée Dr. Carol Greider to do the work in genetics that would ultimately win them both the Nobel Prize in Physiology or Medicine.

Many successful women I know say that consciously learning from mentors helped advance their careers in a big way, while several less successful ones felt the lack of guidance keenly. Over the course of our advertising careers, Nancy and I had some tough, clear-eyed mentors who saw potential in us that we never imagined for ourselves. For me, Mark Hilltout was the game changer. He was my seventh creative director in six years of work and my first professional mentor. And neither of us saw it coming.

"Sylvie and I had a hotel in the Seychelles." Mark, the raconteur was holding court as I walked into the dinner party where I first met him. "David Bowie and his wife used to come and stay with us. We went fishing. I didn't know who he was. I do now, of course. Ha ha." Big laugh. Colorful. Outrageous. Mark had driven Sylvie across Africa in an open-air jeep as a marriage proposal. Did Ogilvy Toronto have an in-house bar? he asked. No? Why not? They did at

Ogilvy Capetown. Was there a tea lady who came around with the cart at three p.m.? No? There was at Ogilvy Hong Kong. He stared at me across the table, dark brown eyes, intense. "Are you Jewish?" he asked me. I nodded. He shook his head thoughtfully. "You must be a good writer. Jewish are good writers." Are you kidding me? Over one meal, I decided Mark was either the best or the worst person I'd ever met, but it didn't matter; I'd taken a few years off to be with Devin and didn't plan to go back into advertising, so I didn't expect to have any reason to know him better.

Then one of my freelance clients decided they needed an ad agency and agreed to let Ogilvy pitch as long as I was brought in as the writer on the business. I wasn't looking for work but agreed to help if I could do it with Nancy, who I'd met a couple of years earlier. Mark wasn't impressed. He glared at me from one end of the long boardroom table in his office. I glared at him from the other end. Pistols at high noon. He said, "At the end of three weeks, if I think you're any good and you find me tolerable, both of which I doubt, I may consider hiring you." *Jerk,* I thought, but said, "I can't imagine wanting to be hired, and I agree that I doubt I'll find you tolerable." Twenty-one days, multiple arm-wrestles and one lost pitch later, Mark persuaded me to accept some summer freelance work and spent the next three months campaigning to keep me. He flattered and cajoled. He gave me any assignment I wanted. Relentless, he brought all his powers of persuasion to bear. "Dahhhling, stay for Nancy. Stay for me. Imagine what we could all do together." I caved, and that was the best decision of my working life.

Mark was the boss I'd always looked for and I loved him for it. A guide, not a dictator, he would offer commentary rather than give orders. "Too many words, dahhhling," the *r* drawn out like pulled taffy, but he left me to find my own solution. It was the right strategy to get me to excel.

Mark judged all creative work on a scale of 1 to 10, with 1 meaning "Why do you have a job?" and 10—"Only God gets a 10"—so it was a scale of 2 to 9, really. His comments on work were brief and clear. A 4 needed work. A 6 could go to clients. If he believed something was a 4 and you thought it was a 6, he'd say, "We're in the business of public opinion. If you can find ten people who agree with you, I'll let you do it your way." If you can find ten who agree with you—Mark was stubborn but not closed.

Listen. Trust your own judgment, but be open to being wrong. Then be gracious. Years later, after the Dove Litmus Test advertising that he'd thought was a 5 or at best a 6, had sold mountains of soap and won multiple awards, he said out of the blue, "Maybe it was a 9. I'd never had a 9 before."

Mark's guidance was pithy and clear. Trust yourself but listen to others. Own the room, but don't make it about you. Critique the work, not the person. If you don't like the situation, change it. Don't use coffee creamer; spend the money for cream. Keep beer in the fridge. Take risks. Bet on people.

Was I conscious of the impact of Mark's counsel on the quality of my work and my resulting career potential? Absolutely. Did I believe I could offer this to someone else—say determined but grammatically challenged Arthur? Who knew?

To save my own neck, I had to learn to grow talent in a hurry. For months, Arthur and I spent hours together, me saying things like, "Move this line here." "That's not your last line. That's your headline." "It's not clear enough." "Take that out. No one but you will ever know it's not there." "Write it again." He wrote it again. And five times after that. Then ten more. He took an evening writing course. I read every word he wrote, and nipped and tucked as surgically as if it were mine. He had plenty to lose. Me too. I went out on a limb for him. And to my surprise and unending gratitude, it paid me back a hundred times over.

And the winner is . . .

My experience with Arthur opened my eyes to the surprising benefits of mentorship. What struck me hardest was this question: Who wins in a mentoring relationship, the giver or the receiver?

It's clear what's in it for the mentored—and I'd experienced that side of the relationship firsthand. Mentors offer guidance, help refine skills, demystify office politics, clarify missteps, save a few endangered limbs from being blown off, serve to explain relationships and dynamics; they embolden and connect.

And the mentor? The person who gives up her time and brain

cells to improving the career of someone else—what about her? In places where mentoring isn't a formal process, many take the view that mentoring is what "nice" people do to earn brownie points in do-gooder heaven. It's a way of—excuse the tired phrase—giving back. And it usually leads to a hand held up in the "stop right there" position and the words, "Thanks, but I already work thirty-two hours a day." Fair enough. It absolutely isn't the right choice for everybody. I might have felt it wasn't the right choice for me if I hadn't experienced its career-boosting power firsthand.

The hours I spent with Arthur paid off. He kept his copywriter business card and I kept mine. (Was my job really on the line? Luckily, I never had to find out.) Next thing we knew, Nancy and I were running Ogilvy's internship program. We started giving "opportunity" projects to younger people in the group so they could get a taste of work that was more demanding. We challenged their ideas so they could learn to tell their stories better. We rehearsed them like film directors before they went into presentations. We mentored them. And they inspired us. It was an organic growth experience for us. Mark called it leadership and said things like, "I'm going to change your title from senior copywriter to group head." We didn't want more responsibility. We were just fine, thank you very much. "No, we'll take a pass," we said. But he insisted. "You're doing the job already. You might as well get paid for it."

What's in it for you?

In advertising, your portfolio is your bargaining chip. The better it is, the more money you make. It's how "creatives" get hired in the first place, so most of our careers are spent strengthening it. We do smarter, fresher work for our clients so that they—and we—stand out. The need for award-winning work leads many creative teams to lobby for the best projects, or if you're in charge of assigning them, to keep them to yourself. The impulse to hold onto the biggest client or to lead the best project is human nature whether you work in finance, engineering, technology or advertising. Impressing the powers that be is always the name of the game.

But Nancy and I invited younger teams to work on projects that were ours, and we gave away things that looked like sure award winners because we wanted to see them grow. Looking back, I guess it could have been career suicide. Except that inadvertently, we started to learn how to do other things, like how to guide talent, share information, understand individual abilities, make decisions about who would benefit from working on a particular project. It taught us to delegate, an especially hard lesson when individual achievement is the key to your success. It never crossed our minds that we were planting a seed for the future. Our personal portfolio was strong. But our track record of developing amazing talent was even more compelling. It set us apart.

Eighteen months or so after I'd started working for him, Mark told me we needed to talk. Uh-oh. At that same boardroom table, he said, "You're soft, yet hahhhd. You know that's what a creative director needs to be. I won't be here forever. You should think about it." Whaaat? I don't know which statement freaked me out more: that he was thinking of leaving or that he put my name and the words "creative director" in the same sentence. What I do know is that until that day, the idea of being a creative director had never crossed my mind. I wasn't interested and wouldn't be for several more years, but the work Nancy and I did in helping other people develop their careers cleared a path for us.

So what's the biggest obstacle to becoming a mentor? For some, it's lack of interest, but mostly it's not enough hours in the day. I get it. I've been there—I'm still there some days. The *Handbook on Women in Business and Management* points out that the relatively few women who are in a position to mentor feel so overwhelmed with workload and the need to be the absolute best at what they're doing that they simply can't make the time.[18] Never mind if they also have families to worry about. And their organizations don't really support them spending their time that way. But what if they, and you, thought of mentoring as an act of enlightened self-interest that could turbocharge your own career development?

Most don't think of mentoring as part of a strategy for success. We didn't either, but for us it was the winning ticket in a lottery we didn't know we'd entered. Nowadays, we call it "selfish mentoring" with a secret little ™ beside it. That sounds like an oxymoron, but it can be the secret sauce. Putting a freakish amount of time and energy into developing talent was the straight line between intern wrangler and chief creative officer. Author Richard Bach's phrase, "You teach best what you most need to learn," was spectacularly true for us. As we mentored others, we learned to lead. I doubt we'd ever have got there on our own.

Whatever the mash-up of nature and nurture, mentoring became our natural element. Not many people see the youngest as the ones who can deliver the goods, but ours did over and over. We threw them in the deep end and then threw them a rope if it looked as if they were going down for the third time. Giving major opportunities, support and credit to people who would normally fetch coffee or be an extra pair of hands for the seniors was unusual, to say the least. It was the hallmark of our leadership style, and it played a crucial role in helping the entire organization have creative success. If the juniors had better ideas, the seniors had to put down their tools and help bring those ideas to life. Yes, there was grumbling, but future leaders were being born in the process.

The devaluing of mentoring and how it hurts women

Once upon a time, mentoring was an education strategy in business, a training tool—think Mickey Mouse in "The Sorcerer's Apprentice." It hasn't been so long since people learned through apprenticeship. Junior people were in the hands of thoughtful senior people until the training wheels were ready to come off. But in modern business life, mentoring has become a largely voluntary exercise, something you do purely out of the goodness of your heart. In a 2011 article in *The Atlantic*, Elli Sharef of the start-up HireArt says, "They [companies] don't want to train people on the job anymore. There are just too many people looking for work for companies to waste time on someone who can't start, ready to go, on the first day. Candidates are left to fend for themselves."[19] It's time for a reframe.

In many places, mentoring, if it exists at all, is organic rather than organized. Everywhere, there's a whole lot more sinking than swimming. Cathy Preston of Preston Human Capital Group confirmed this. "Over a decade ago, there was a huge halt in all forms of learning and development in most big companies," she said. "It's tough to find senior people who know what they're doing if they've been in those roles for less than ten years. They haven't been taught."

Given that "no one is managing my career" is one of the top reasons that good people leave a company, the money "saved" by not investing in employees is a false economy. It can cost $75,000 to replace a $50,000 employee when you consider invisible hits like lost productivity, knowledge and training. The Center for American Progress estimates that a new hire can cost 10 to 30 percent more in salary alone.[20] This should give a company pause.

The HR director of a major global corporation recently said that while his organization has a manual for teaching people how to mentor, getting them to actually do it is left to chance; an employee has to put her hand up or the boss has to think to offer it. It's not built into the system. Letting the chips fall—now there's a strategy for talent development. Increasingly, people are expected to walk into leadership jobs without leadership skills.

For women, this drop in organized mentoring is especially brutal. Mentoring helps you build leadership skills in a low-pressure, organic way months or years before you get the title—which is perfect, because we tend not to raise our hand for an opportunity unless we've proved to ourselves beyond a reasonable doubt that we can do it. Deirdre Woods, interim executive director at the University of Pennsylvania's Open Learning Initiative, has observed that women "need to know 80 percent, 90 percent of their current job before they feel ready to step into a new role . . . Men start thinking of their next promotion right after they start their new promotion."[21]

Chris Tardio of The Lookinglass has seen this phenomenon at play in the careers of the high-powered women she coaches. "Women think they have to tick all of the boxes of qualifications for a job before they're comfortable accepting an opportunity, whereas men will apply if they have 30 percent of the skills for the job."

Mentoring builds mojo. Nancy and I are living proof of this. Neither of us thought we had "the right stuff" when the creative director opportunity fairy came knocking for the fifth time. But when we looked back over years of making stars out of newbies, we realized that we were further along than we gave ourselves credit for—which ultimately led us to "yes."

Mentoring a new career

In 2011, when Nancy and I were getting serious about leaving Ogilvy, we put ourselves through a crazily informal "What do you love most and how can you earn a living doing it?" process. Sheets upon sheets of scribbles, ideas and idea starters, some semi–fleshed out, others mere bony skeletons. What did we love when all the flash and film and awards fuss was out of the picture? People. Making them better, letting them make us better. Light bulb. A wiggling tadpole of an idea that might have something going for it. But what if we were the only ones who saw a lack of leadership ability in a generation that had grown up as training and mentoring vanished?

We polled creative directors of ad agencies from London to Argentina for a reality check. Most said they didn't have the time for training or mentoring; they were strapped for cash, overworked, understaffed. Every day was a high-wire act. Most felt that the series of economic downturns had left them unable to devote any energy to raising talent, and they were filled with frustration that their teams didn't appear to be growing up on their own. They couldn't see future leaders within their own ranks. They admitted to poaching from other agencies when they needed seriously senior people, hiring for the need, a much more expensive way to build a team than developing the talent they had. There was a theme: "We're in trouble. Where's the next round of leaders?" The same challenges were everywhere. We'd identified a genuine need.

On a steamy New York summer day in a noisy, open-air café, we put the tadpole down on the table in front of Alnoor Ladha, ex-ad guy, passionate human rights activist, social movement catalyst, superb business strategist, and our young spirit guide. Together, we sketched out a possible future on that famous advertising cliché, the back of a napkin. Okay, a placemat. Eureka! Our new business was a bunch of boxes and circles and arrows and lines with some stick people in the middle, each box a creative tool, each circle an experience, all held together by a crazy, patchwork quilt of brilliant, creative people from many fields, who would help students become better leaders. It wouldn't feel like learning so much as a mind-blowing, life-altering series of revelations. But would it work? A creativity-infused mentoring-teaching-leadership consultancy? Who would pay for that at a time when all these things had been excised from budgets like the bruise on an apple?

And then, a godsend.

"Why the Average Barista Gets More Training than Most Agency Staffers."[22] That was the startling headline that leapt off the pages of *Adweek*, a leading trade publication, in March 2011. The chickens had come home to roost; the worm had turned; reaping, sowing; the choices advertising had made were biting it in the ass—pick your well-worn idiom. Overnight, the lack of well-educated, capable, trustworthy leadership talent went from dirty little secret to front-page news, and employee education became the hottest topic in our industry. As the mea culpas flew, ad agency and holding company heads one-upped each other as to who would be first to bring it back. It was a tipping point. To our surprise, not only were ad agencies looking for new ways to develop the quality of their leaders, so were marketers, retailers, banks, architects and tech firms.

Over the course of our years of mentoring, there were those who said, "Why bother? They'll just leave." That's not our experience. It made our agency the shiniest object for up-and-comers. Young people, without two cents to rub together, turned down actual decent-paying jobs to take our considerably less lucrative internship because they knew their foundations would be stronger and their career paths swifter. They often stayed with the agency longer than they otherwise would have. We developed a reputation for turning out talented, accomplished young people who could take on the jobs of the much more seasoned. Our interns won top awards at international awards shows—gold Cannes Lions, One Show Pencils and Grand Clios—and they weren't even employed yet. They were green, but in our environment, they flourished. Arthur, the guy from accounting, has a shelf full of awards to his credit, became a creative director and is an active mentor himself. Many of our protégés have become exceptional creative directors; some have opened their own agencies. Their success has enhanced ours—give and take all the way. Our interest in helping others along also led us to create the book in your hands, and ultimately Swim, our creative leadership lab.

So you want to be a mentor . . .

When I was in high school and struggling with a homework question, I'd moan about it to my father, asking him to help me answer it. He'd say, "Tell me the problem." And then he'd say, "Now tell me again." Eyes rolling, I'd point out that I'd just told him the problem twice and what I needed was for him to help find the solution. "Tell me in a different way," he'd say, as if I hadn't spoken. Somehow, in the repeated rephrasing of the question, a light would go on in my head. I could suddenly see, if not the answer itself, a path to getting there. As I got older, he helped me with my business and personal life in exactly the same way. He refused to do the work for me, but through his experience, wise counsel and annoying nudging to look at every problem from different angles, he continued to be my guide.

He never told me what to do; he merely asked the questions that allowed me to open my own door to the solutions. He saw things in me that I didn't see. He had faith I didn't have. My dad was my first true mentor. Mark guided me in exactly the same way.

So what does it take to be a great mentor? Rebecca's story gives some important clues. She works in a large company where it's hard to differentiate yourself, especially as a woman. Lacking a big team, she changed the way she spent her remaining budget: she employed more people for less money. Yes, she built a team mostly of millennials—no small challenge. She experimented with how to get the most out of them. Sometimes they work in pairs, sometimes alone, and occasionally as a whole group. She gives them lots of feedback and encourages them to do the same for each other. Her results have been surprising even to her. Despite the millennial reputation of being "self-centered, lazy and demanding," Rebecca hasn't seen any of that.[23] In managing the "unmanageables," she's developed her leadership muscles and is now a green dot blinking brightly on the company's radar.

Like Rebecca, you have to think of it as a full-blown, ring-on-the-finger engagement, not a casual one-night stand. Set clear goals and criteria for judging the outcomes, even in the most informal version of the relationship. Remember that mentors listen; they don't just talk. To figure out how they could do their best, Rebecca kept mixing up the way her team worked. If her way wasn't the right way, there were new things to be explored.

I read an adage once that said, "mentoring is a way of using someone's hindsight as your foresight." Attitudes age, but wisdom doesn't. If your radar is well tuned to the needs of your mentee, you'll find the most helpful way to use and convey your experience. As in any relationship, everyone needs to get something out of it or it's doomed to fail. Remember, you don't have to be old to be a mentor. Younger people know a whole lot about a whole lot, and they can be brilliant advisors, especially in these digital days. The first step to mentoring is to put up your hand. Your foresight can change an entire career path, as Mark's did for us. More important, it can change your own.

Maybe building your career on the backs of juniors looks self-serving, but it isn't if your interest is genuine and you're helping to build their careers. Few women mentor with a motive to advance. In my experience, most of us do it because we recognize the need for women mentors and truly want to help—which is what makes it such a brilliant and subtle leg up. But what's in it for us can't be bought: we learn as we teach, over time proving to ourselves that we have the skills and experience we need to lead. For us, mentoring others didn't start out as a selfish career strategy, but it helped us more than we ever thought possible. You can get started today. Just channel my dad.

Good things come to those who wait.

In the Google cafeteria, people are milling about looking for a seat. A chorus of "Mind if I sit here?" and "Is this taken?" bounces softly around a room vibrating with energy and the constant hum of conversation. Nancy and I have been sitting with Sabrina Geremia, Canada's managing director of integrated solutions, for a whole seven or eight minutes and she's already introduced us to three different people. "You guys should talk," she suggests. "Maybe you can find ways to work together." We're just here for the cinnamon buns and a catch-up, but this natural-born connector can't help doing her thing. She tells us how a young woman came to the table where she and a few others were eating lunch a few weeks earlier, and asked, "May I sit?" A half-hour later, as people started to leave, the young woman turned to Sabrina and asked if she could book an hour with her the following week. Would Sabrina be her mentor?

"Next week? Why don't we just talk now?" Disappointment flashed across the woman's face. She declined nervously—she wasn't ready. You could almost hear the screeching as the girl put the brakes on her chance to build the relationship. At the speed of their business, trying to get an hour of Sabrina's time is like trying to grab a handful of water, which has driven her to take drastic, and brilliant, measures. "I've started minute-mentoring." She laughs. "I want people to think about what they want from me so that when they see me in the elevator, they can say, 'Do you have a minute to talk about this?' 'This' being whatever is on their minds: a project, an idea, a situation, even a little career chat. I encourage women to grab me when I'm getting a coffee or picking up a snack in the micro-kitchen for ten minutes. Chances are I'll say, 'Let's take ten and talk about it right now.'"

Sabrina is the model of a modern mentor. She's open and generous and makes herself available in bite-sized chunks of time, because full hours don't exist. Yet women, and especially young women, hold back because it feels too opportunistic. So they wait till help offers itself or until they've gathered up their courage in both hands. They know that they need to be proactive to advance their careers, but they don't know how, so they wait: if ever there was a rule that needed breaking, it's this one. Sabrina's colleague had the right idea in looking for a mentor, but she didn't have the confidence to grab the lift when it appeared. If she had taken the offered hand, though, she'd have quickly discovered that her boss puts a lot of energy into helping Google women understand how to get the career supercharge they need, while at the same time handing them the keys to their own power.

Is it socialization? Our natural instincts? Whatever the reason, too many women believe that good things come to those who wait. Ever spent time in a classroom? A large body of research shows that boys are much more likely than girls to blurt out the answer when the teacher poses a question. And because they tend to be early responders, they often dominate classroom discussions, especially in a university setting.[24] When it comes to the workplace, woman have to learn to blurt—and by "blurt," we mean ask for help when they need it—and be willing to seize help no matter what form it comes in.

Many women, myself included, find it tough to ask for help, in case it looks bad on them. What really looks bad is turning away from the thing that can speed your education and hoist you up. Learning how to find people to guide you and unlock doors can be the difference between a career that rocks and one that plods.

Mentors and sponsors: why two is better than one
In the last chapter, we looked at what *being* a mentor can do for your career. But having mentors and sponsors is just as mission critical, so it's worth pausing for a quick definition, because while

you may hear the terms used interchangeably, they're not actually the same thing. *The Guardian*'s Allyson Zimmermann wrote that mentors are career developers and sponsors are career accelerators.[25] The nonprofit research firm dedicated to the advancement of women, Catalyst, defines them more prosaically: sponsors are advocates in positions of authority who use their influence intentionally to help others advance, while mentors provide advice, feedback and coaching.[26] Mentors can be with you throughout your career. Sponsors come into the story later. Each can have a role in guiding you to your personal destination.

But if my work is outstanding, shouldn't that be enough? If only it were that simple. Of course, your work should be stellar. But learning how to talk to the higher-ups, successfully manage through conflicts, rise above the bad days and see the big picture are all equally important skills that usually require lessons of the been-there-done-that variety, which is why the people we choose and those who choose us along the way are just as important.

I didn't have any kind of mentoring in my early years and I think it decelerated my progress. I figured if I typed my fingers to the bone and did a good job, that's all there was to it. I'd been typing for several years when Mark Hilltout came into the picture, lending some shape and direction to my journey. Mark was no pussycat. As you've probably already noticed, he was tough and exacting. His feedback could be cutting. He pushed, pushed, pushed: "Is that all there is? Try again." He demanded excellence, and when we pulled it off, he pushed us further still. It wasn't easy, but it was helluva fun, as Mark would say.

There's a lot you can learn only on the job. We've seen what happens when people get into high places without the help of mentors. They often don't know how to treat people or how to have hard conversations. Mark and others were our school away from school. They kicked us into doing all kinds of things that changed our futures, like learning how to hire and how to make tough calls; they showed us the fine line between criticizing the work and criticizing the person. They sent us to sit on awards show juries, which for creative teams helps to boost your credibility and profile almost overnight, though I didn't see it that way at first. I had one bad judging experience early on, where a jury of men couldn't see the cleverness in a TV ad aimed specifically at women. I thought the ad was killer and said so. They met my comments with their fingers in their ears, and I decided I never wanted to judge again. The next time I was invited, my instincts were to say a big, fat no. My mentor pointed out that I couldn't change things from the outside, and that work that appealed to women would never be rewarded if that change didn't happen. I desperately wanted to boycott, but he made a lot of sense. I did it, and this jury—again mostly men—was much more open to my female viewpoint. That much-needed perspective—delivered at precisely the right time—not only opened new doors for me but also helped me realize just how much power I had to start making the changes I wanted to see.

"Mentoring helps women move more swiftly in an organization, especially a large one," says executive recruiter Cathy Preston. If you think that mentoring is important only if you're trying to rise up within a large organization, think again. Big, small, self-employed, we can all find the help and use it to have greater success. Mentorship even has a role to play for women entrepreneurs. "A lack of early advisors" is one of the biggest reasons women entrepreneurs raise 70 percent less capital than men do, according to Lesa Mitchell of the Ewing Marion Kauffman Foundation, a large, private institution in the United States that focuses on entrepreneurship and education. Mentors coach us over many hurdles.

Where have all the mentors gone?

In my experience, most women understand the value mentors bring, yet many still don't have them. The informal networks that guys have make starting these kinds of relationships easier and more organic. For women, it's more awkward. Chasing after somebody and asking them to "be your mentor" seems too needy. On top of that, many of us feel more at home with peers, so we don't always seek out the people "way up there" who might lend a hand up. A penny dropped for me when Sharon MacLeod, vice president of marketing at Unilever, said, "Men manage up. Women manage across or down." A high-speed film of all the women I know flashed before my eyes, and I realized that, in the main, it was true. Their internal networks were their friends. Ditto for me for a long time. Women worry that it'll as if like we're kissing up if we actively try to connect with the higher-ups. Instead, we wait for them to come to us, and it just doesn't happen. Those people aren't wandering around with fishing rods, looking to hook themselves someone to mentor. So we're always the one that got away.

Another reason women don't put much elbow grease into finding strong mentors is that they put a lot of their energy into other things, like running the United Way fund-raising drive and organizing the Christmas party. Surely a good team-player contribution like that will get them noticed. What it actually does is split their energies to the point of self-sabotage. Party committees are helpful and fun. They're a good way to get to know people when you're starting out, but you have to learn when to move on and think about adding in some of the supportive relationships that will serve you in the long term.

Surprisingly, mentoring itself can be a stumbling block if you're not careful. Nancy and I learned a ton from doing it, but then there's overdoing it. Suzanne West, a program manager at the manufacturing company Textron Inc. who supervises 350 people, told *The Wall Street Journal* that she'd never turned down a request to mentor someone and had, in fact, mentored up to ten women a year since 2008. A 360-degree performance review revealed that—*horrors*—she was actually mentoring too much, and it was holding back her own career. Suzanne dialed it down to just two women and turned some of her attention back to herself; she asked some of the senior execs in her company to mentor her.[27]

According to the Dallas-based leadership consultancy ELI Group, about a third of the participants in its Leadership Lab for Women receive more than two dozen requests each year to mentor junior colleagues.[28] So many women would love female mentors—the similar obstacle course thing is a big draw—but they aren't falling out of the sky. The numbers of women with enough experience to be really valuable to other women just aren't that high. Men are still the most likely candidates for anyone seeking support. No surprise there. There are simply more of them in the influential positions, and they have a tremendous amount to offer. No one understands the system the way they do. That guidance is invaluable.

But looking to men for mentoring can come with its own set of challenges. For example, they aren't always willing to do it. They feel that they don't understand women's issues well enough or they don't actually think there's a problem. And then, there's the men-coaching-women dynamic, which can be complicated for a reason you might not guess: it makes guys nervous. We may be absolutely fine with it, but they find it . . . well, uncomfortable. They worry that the relationship will be misunderstood, especially if the man is older, which, let's be honest, is usually the case. One CEO told me that he had a senior exec walk away from mentoring women because his wife had said, "Why all these girls?" In the company of her male mentors, Kathleen Warner has been mistaken for the wife, the assistant, the junior. "People make weird assumptions, so men say, 'I can't spend time with you. People will talk,'" says Kathleen, who is the founding chief operating officer at Startup America Partnership, a U.S.-based network of start-up initiatives for entrepreneurs. So men don't readily put themselves forward to help women out unless they've signed on to a formal program. One CEO had this solution: he would meet with mentees, male or female, only in the office, during regular office hours, in the open. If you treat everyone the same way, nothing can be misinterpreted.

Unfortunately, most organizations don't support the "coaching" skill set for employees. No one gets paid extra for lending a guiding hand. Add to that the lack of a formal system and the drain on people's time, and it becomes easy to see why so few, male or female, are racing to do it.

So what do you do when your company doesn't offer it? Cathy Preston recommends that women look out in the big, wide world. Seek those who have experience where you don't. Look for the seeing eye dogs you can trust to guide you through the business environment in different ways: your university economics professor; Uncle Steven, the family entrepreneur; Yumi, the female COO of a major tech company who spoke at a conference and then wound up sitting next to you at lunch. I kid you not. These things really can happen. In 2004, Karen Phillips, the current chief executive of The Fed, a social care charity in Manchester, England, wrote a letter to Mark Adlestone, chairman of Beaverbrooks, one of the United Kingdom's top four companies to work in, asking him to be her mentor. They'd never met, but he called her, they talked and he agreed. He's been her mentor for almost nine years.[29] There are a bunch of different ways women can fill the hole left by budget cuts and lack of commitment to their specific development. If you can't find it under your own roof, don't wait. Grab help wherever and whenever it's offered. Do it for yourselves, sisters.

Mentor for hire

Doing it for themselves is how a number of women discovered—and hired—Bill Johnson. The former CEO of McDonald's Canada had been working as a business coach and professional mentor for a couple of years before he realized that he was working with a disproportionately high number of women. They had been looking for help and couldn't find it, so they reached into their wallets. Bill knows a thing or two about mentoring: "I was never without a mentor from the time I was young till I retired from the CEO spot. I had four of them. The first three were guys, older than me. And the best of the lot was Mary Anne Drummond, who was the head of HR at McDonald's. I was the CEO by that time, but you never know everything and you can always use a frank point of view. Most men have a hard time having a woman as a mentor. We're not open enough and you have to feel comfortable. What can I say? They're missing out."

If Bill had his way, everyone would have at least two mentors, one male, one female, but senior women leaders are hard to find, so think about what can work for them, not just what they can do for you: "I know this person is approachable and would give me great advice. How can I do this in a way that makes it easy for her?" Try suggesting Sabrina Geremia's minute-mentoring approach.

Link arms with other women

When you work in an environment where a male pilot feels free to say to a female pilot, "If God had meant women to fly, he'd have made the sky pink instead of blue," or a passenger says, "She doesn't look like a captain," and asks to see your credentials, first you want to strangle the insensitive asses. Then you want to make sure it never happens to you again. That's what first drew helicopter pilot Lorena Knapp, the current head of The Ninety-Nines, to the women pilots' mentoring association. The Ninety-Nines were started in 1929 by Jenny Beatty, an airline captain who saw the lack of progress of women in her industry. Jenny recognized that if there were going to be more women captains, they needed to create a support system. The first ninety-nine women included Amelia Earhart.[30] Men knew nothing about it.

The now less secret society operates on a "start as a learner, end as a leader" mentoring model. Their enviable three-part program starts with you as the mentee, evolves to mentor and mentee working together, and ultimately leads to the mentee becoming a mentor to someone else. All women pilots are doing better because of it but not just because of the skills they gain. The Ninety-Nines is a "boys' club" for women: there's someone to advocate for you, to walk your résumé over if there's a spot to be filled. That kind of support is how a whole lot of hiring gets done, regardless of industry. And for women pilots, it's led to women busting down doors that were previously bolted shut. Chances are you're not a helicopter pilot. You might not even work in a male-dominated industry, but no matter where you work, peer support can be a form of mentoring. And together, you might be inspired to start your own mentorship program.

Keep angels on your shoulder (they'll help you fly)

What if you lived your life with a group of angels on your shoulder that you could call on whenever you needed support or guidance? Picture those same angels with good business sense, decades of business experience, no obligation to love you, and a gift for straight talk. Now dub this a personal advisory board (PAB).

Denise Pickett, executive vice president and CEO of U.S. Loyalty at American Express, is passionate when she talks about her personal advisory board. "When I was going through the process for both the country manager job in Canada and then later the relocation to the U.S., I wasn't supposed to tell anyone when I first knew the outcome, but they'd been so important to me during the process, I wanted them to know what happened. So we agreed to a code. I'd just put 'yes' in the subject line of an email to them. I wanted to acknowledge their role in getting me there." Denise ranks her PAB high on her "most important" list. Not right up there with husband and kids but definitely above the family dog. It's become such a big part of her world that she factored it into her decision to move to the United States when the opportunity arose for a big career jump. "I can't imagine life without it. Luckily, the group said we'd work it out."

In Denise's PAB, all the women advise each other. They have helped each other through every imaginable career challenge: new business ideas and launches, new jobs, relocation, promotion. If you can think of it, they've faced it. And they've been at it for over ten years. They're objective and challenging, and hold each other to account. Over time, the group has transcended the hardcore professional; they've become each other's most trusted personal and professional advisors. (Trust is such a critical component of the relationship that Denise wouldn't even talk to me without their say-so.)

"We were thrown together at the Judy Project. It was what we had in common. It makes a difference to have something in common from the get-go, I think. And it builds from there." The Judy Project. The name alone highlights why it's one of a kind. Designed specifically for high-potential women by the University of Toronto's Rotman School of Management, the Judy Project has put 250 women through its tough, generous, entertaining, educational weeklong boot camp over the last eleven years. And every group goes away connected, each other's personal advisory board, giving the gift of business savvy, a thirty-thousand-foot view of the world and the kind of advice you can never get from people who know you too well.

But that's only one way to build the support system you need, as I told Lucy when she sought me out after a speech Nancy and I gave in San Francisco. She was all but pulling out her curly hair as she described the frustration of being the only senior woman in a digital media company, and harder still, the only one over thirty-five. None of her colleagues had been working long enough to help her with her challenges on the job or in her career. We pulled aside a couple of chairs and started to sketch out a plan. Did she need a mentor? A coach? A personal advisory board? "That's it. That's what I want. And I want to put it together myself." We made a list of people that included someone she knew from a different type of digital company (to avoid accidental corporate espionage), a much-admired boss from a previous job for some wisdom, a British friend of mine who worked in a similar company but in a completely different country (so she wouldn't be competing for a job). I offered her someone from my network, who gave the idea an enthusiastic thumbs up. Not everyone has the time, but if you put out your hand, it's amazing who will reach out to take it.

Once you've decided what kind of PAB you want, you can design your own rules for how to get the most out of it. Will you have one retreat a year and three "lifelines" meetings once a quarter, two group videoconferences, a conversation once a season with the person you need most, and a dinner with the group when everyone brings fresh eyes? The beauty of engineering your own system is that it's up to you how it goes.

Form a circle

Have you heard of mentoring circles? These are popular everywhere, from the Massachusetts Bar Association to religious organizations to archivists and scientists. In other words, they have a whole lot of traction in places where it might be tough to find an individual mentor. Like PABs, mentoring circles give you access to more than one set of eyes and advice. In some cases, each person involved is both a mentor and a mentee. Your mentor might be older than you or younger, more experienced or less, in the same industry or not. The circle might be organized like a military operation or designed much more casually. One senior lawyer found that some of her biggest aha moments have come from much more junior lawyers. Chemistry has everything to do with these groups working out, like any other mentoring relationship. As for having a mentor outside your day-to-day experience, a lot of people prefer it. No baggage means they can't get tripped up in the fine points of what you do. That objectivity is like coming up from under water after holding your breath to the point of bursting—incredibly freeing.

Find a spirit guide

It sounds all spooky or New Age, but you'd be surprised how many people use ghost mentors. We did. After we'd been banging our heads against the wall, trying to come up with ad ideas, Nancy and I would occasionally turn to a ghost for help: How would Jamie Oliver think about it, or John Lennon? What about Oprah? We turned to painters, musicians, scientists, anyone who might unstick our brains and liberate us to look at things differently. Social media strategist Jennifer Kane wrote about how conjuring Seth Godin has taught her resilience, civility and how to continue the search for a purple cow.

Novelist Andromeda Romano-Lax was struggling with a finished but unsatisfactory draft of a novel. So she put pen to paper and wrote herself the feedback and career advice she imagined getting from several of her favorite authors. Her imaginary Michael Chabon shared his own story of an unpublished second book and commiserated with her difficulty in deciding whether to rewrite or cut bait. Contrarian, imaginary Philip Roth had no interest in her book but talked about the inspiration that comes from adversity, while imaginary Virginia Woolf wished she would aim to be more innovative, for heaven's sake! They weren't the kindest bunch, but they gave Andromeda a whole different perspective, even helping her to accept failure if that was the outcome and to work to "fail better," to quote non-imaginary Samuel Beckett.

Poet and professor Emily Wall went a more practical route as she worked on her latest book of poetry. Frustrated with the lack of guidance available to someone who works alone—entrepreneurs, take note—she found two writers online who seemed a good fit: a woman in Washington state, and a young man with a completely different life experience from Emily's own: he's unmarried, has no children and lives in remotest Alaska. The three of them set expectations, defined goals and roles and kicked it off with a teleconference. Then Emily sent each mentor fifteen poems a week for eight weeks. Word docs flying back and forth between the city and the forest. Embedded comments. Keen observations the last Friday of the month. In her blog post on the subject, Emily wrote, "This mentorship has been electrifying. What a gift to have someone rattle me awake in this way."[31]

What a perfect description of the role and responsibility of a mentor: someone who rattles you awake and holds your feet to the fire; one part educator, one part supporter, one part strict taskmaster, one part advisor. Shake your cocktail to your own taste.

The lawyer who said she'd learned a ton from younger lawyers was on to something big: your mentor doesn't have to be older than you, as we learned in spades when Lara Palmer took us to task a few months after we started running the creative department. She caught us off guard. Lara worked for us. She was several years younger. And less experienced. Hello? Respect? But she had what it took to read us the riot act: "You guys said that your door is always open and that you want to hear our thoughts. Well, you're blowing it. This team creative director experience is freaking people out. You're disagreeing like bad parents in front of the kids, and they're playing you off against each other—'Well, *Mom* said it was okay'—and you don't even see it." Nancy and I had started our new job thinking we'd just keep working as a team and that would be just peachy. Talk about not having a clue. Often, we weren't in the same place at the same time. So one of us would say something to our teams and, hours later, the other would say something else, because we hadn't had time to share our thoughts. It was so confusing for our group. Lara shone a light on a reality we couldn't see. She became our ongoing reality check and radically changed our approach for the better. The idea that mentorship doesn't have to be all God-like and Come From Above was a revelation.

In her riveting book *Willful Blindness*, Margaret Heffernan talks about the rising importance of reverse-mentoring relationships, like the one we stumbled into. Forward-looking companies are starting to invite young people to comment on how their managers are managing. It's scary all around, but a great boss can have her ears and eyes opened and grow because of it, especially these days. In this digital, social world, the young people coming in understand the landscape far better than the people they work for. It takes courage for a young person to offer guidance to a boss, so make sure they feel safe to be honest. Make sure to say thanks.

Though mentorship can come through many doors, typically, it's still male-led and senior to junior. "Which comes with a surprising benefit," Geeta Sheker, director of the Initiative for Women in Business and head of The Judy Project at the Rotman School, told me with a satisfied smile. "Your male mentor learns from you." As that guy helps you find your way around the world you're in, your experience paints a vivid picture for him of what women are up against. As your mentor sees your world more clearly, he becomes more open to the kinds of change that move women forward. Each of you is translating for the other. It's the business equivalent of fair trade.

Mentoring isn't a one-way street. The best relationships have an element of give and take. Mark mentored us; we raised up his next generation. We ran the internship program; interns did gorgeous work that was way beyond their years and won awards for the agency. Lara was our ear to the ground; we helped her grow into a leader.

At last, a word from our sponsor . . .

At a certain stage in your career, you may discover that mentoring just isn't enough and what you really need is a sponsor, or a champion—a career-maker. Sponsors are well-connected senior people who sit at the decision-making table and have the power and influence to open doors for you. When it comes to advancing to senior positions, sponsors are the secret weapon. Here are snapshots of how sponsors affected the paths of three very successful women by seeing them for who they were, recognizing what they could do and stepping up on their behalf, which doesn't happen for women every day.

Susannah Aliker, a former managing director at Credit Suisse, had a "fantastic champion"—a long-serving, senior ex-marine who had worked his way up the ranks of the organization and earned plenty of cred along the way. "He was terrifically self-confident and that made him incredibly supportive. Because of his stature in the organization, he wouldn't hesitate to say, 'Okay, it might be a bit of a stretch, but Susie could take on that role.'" In getting behind Susannah, her sponsor had a dramatic impact on her career. In her part of the bank, women made up 8 percent of the total number of managing directors—just 14 out of roughly 150. Among the women, there was every permutation: single, married with no children, divorced. Susannah was the only one who was married, married to the same person and had kids—four of them. These days, that's practically an army. Not many people would look at a mother of four and say, "Give that woman a bigger shot." But that's what a sponsor does. Her boss was someone who judged by results and she delivered, so he delivered for her. She describes herself as having "had the right boss at a critical point in my career. He knew what he didn't do well, and I was good at all the things he was less good at. We worked very complementarily because he was confident and promoted me to others."

Kate James, chief of corporate affairs at Pearson, Inc., an international learning company, has a similar story. "It's had everything to do with my success. When I worked at Standard Chartered bank, the CEO, Mervyn Davies, put me on the board of a bank acquisition in Pakistan. He was really serious about career paths for women. I had no experience in a market like that. He said, 'I value you because you have a good understanding of the public affairs piece but also of the strategy for taking this bank forward.'" Clearly, Kate had the chops, but how many people would take a risk on an untested woman in an unfamiliar market? Champions make a huge difference.

"I wish more women understood the importance of sponsorship," Denise Pickett said, and described the morning her phone rang and a very senior male colleague said to her, "You have to go for it no matter how much of a long shot you are."

He was recommending that Denise apply to be the first Canadian to run the entire Canadian operation of American Express. *Long shot indeed*, she thought. *What are the odds?* AmEx has a system of levels, and Denise was two levels down from the country manager job. The guy continued, "You have a chance here, but you have to go in like it's yours to lose." Hers to lose? The thought would've never crossed her mind, not when she'd just been promoted sixteen months earlier, and two levels seemed like the Grand Canyon. The previous three country managers had jumped sideways. Denise was sure it was too early for her, but when the very same sponsors who'd given her her previous promotion asked if she was interested, what could she say but "Of course I am"?

They put her on the slate with the other candidates. It was one grueling interview after another. One on one. Two boards of directors. Eight times over, Denise raised her hand for the chance to do a job that she never would've guessed would be offered.

"A true sponsor takes a risk, plays a chit for you. They are making a major investment in you, putting their reputation on the line. If you don't deliver, it comes back to bite them. And more than one of them weighed in on my behalf."

Denise observes that even if women do have sponsors, they tend to stop at one, while most men aim for three. What do they get that we're not seeing? For starters, sponsorship mostly happens in "the shadows," so many women don't really know much about it and that keeps Denise talking it up wherever she goes. She lets women know what's in it for them and what they need to do to get it. There is a way to be seen, she tells them, even in a large company. There are ways to avoid being passed over. Women's eyes fly open as the light dawns.

Another reason women have fewer sponsors than men is because women invest so heavily in the relationship that it takes longer for it to fully bake. The connections are deeper, but that comes with a trap. If you only have one sponsor and that person says bye-bye to the company, you're back to "Go" without collecting two hundred dollars. And starting over isn't easy.

Unlike mentors, who can be sought out, sponsors choose you because you've shown what you're made of. You can't go shopping for them; sponsorship has to be earned. Susannah Aliker and Kate James developed deep skill sets, showed tons of initiative and delivered big time. Denise Pickett volunteered for tough assignments, moved laterally across business units just to learn more about how things worked and got to know many more people because of it, and they her. When those people moved to bigger jobs, it created new opportunities for Denise, because they knew what kind of person she was and what kind of results they could expect. Along the way, these women acquired champions, as can you.

Denise uses the phrase "earned and owned" to describe sponsoring. You know what "earned" means, but "owned"? "Owning" is thinking about the person who has acted with courage and faith on your behalf, and recognizing the debt. For Denise, it takes the form of hundreds of handwritten thank-you notes a year.

Whenever something good happens—a move or a cool assignment—she writes a thank-you to the sponsor she knows was behind it. No one goes around saying, "I'm so-and-so's sponsor and I'm going to put her forward for this opportunity," or "I'm your sponsor. Look what I'm doing for you." It's all much more subtle, but you know it when it happens and thanks is in order. After Sabrina Geremia was promoted to director at Google, she discovered she'd had a sponsor for years without knowing it. A woman who had been watching her progress and seen her passion for developing Women@Google had put a word in with the right people at the right time. Now Sabrina and Denise and Kate are all doing the same for the women coming up behind them. As Kate James says, we have a big responsibility in our roles as champions for the next generation.

Ignorance is not bliss when it comes to sponsorship. Things entirely left to chance tend not to happen. I love these words from Louis Pasteur: "Chance favors the prepared mind." Women need to think about how to be valuable, and to quote my old boss Tony Houghton, how to also "be seen to be valuable." With some raised consciousness, and intent, women can diversify their group of sponsors through their own efforts.

All companies, almost regardless of size, have their share of backroom jockeying for opportunity that's invisible to most people. But your sponsor will keep an eye out and advocate on your behalf to ensure that you're getting in on opportunities that will stretch, challenge and ultimately develop you. Chances are good your sponsor won't be your direct boss but someone even more senior. In the networking chapter, we'll give you some pointers on how to develop these relationships, but for now it's enough to know that your career needs them.

As young women, we wait for mentors to come our way. As experienced ones, we wait for the big promotions, and for sponsors to find us. Mentoring has a pivotal role to play in building confidence, developing understanding, learning to problem solve. Having a sponsor is like strapping an engine to your career and pressing "blastoff." Both require you to invest time, effort and a lot of chutzpah. Enough with the waiting—good things come to those who go for it.

Nice girls don't get in your face.

At age fourteen, Sandra Shamas realized she needed to be a boy. Told by her guidance counselor that archeology, her declared goal, was "no work for girls," she felt there was a way around this hurdle. From that point forward, Sandra tapped into her inner boy, the part of her that was "assertive, strong, forthright, open." She got the signal: her feminine qualities were weak.

By sheer will, the pragmatic teen reached deep for what she felt she needed to get what she wanted, though one can guess she was never exactly the chiffon- and lavender-wearing type at any age. She told me, "I was always a tomboy." Once she decided to really commit to what she saw as the male pattern of navigating in the world, she found she was getting her way, way more often. But her "un-feminine" behavior sometimes caused great consternation for her Lebanese parents and alienated others who found her ratcheted-up assertiveness inappropriate. Young Sandra was caught in what research firm Catalyst calls "the double bind." When it comes to being assertive, women are "damned if they don't and doomed if they do."

Catalyst found that when women conform to gender stereotypes and behave in a caring, nurturing or caretaking way, we're seen as incompetent and soft—and therefore unqualified for top jobs. But if we display behavior that doesn't conform with stereotypical feminine behavior—we take charge, influence our superiors, or delegate—we're considered too tough and basically unlikable.[32]

It gets worse. A crushingly depressing 2012 Yale University study led by psychology professor Victoria Brescoll found that the cliché of men disliking assertiveness in professional women is essentially true.[33] A *Daily Mail* (UK) article says that based on the study, "female employees who want to succeed in the workplace should keep their mouths shut."[34] The study found that women who spoke up frequently were seen as less competent than their quieter peers. Meanwhile, men who spoke up were usually considered *more* competent.

The author of the study told the *Daily Mail* that "when men talk a lot and they have power, people want to reward them either by hiring them, voting for them, or just giving them more power and responsibility at work. But when women do it, they are seen as being too domineering, too presumptuous." She went on to say, "Women perceive this [double standard], and that's why they temper how much they talk."

Janet and I didn't need the Yale study to tell us that women, from a young age, get the message to tone it down, put on a smile and leave assertiveness to the boys, because it *so* doesn't become you. Never mind the businessmen; this message can come from a parent or a teacher of either gender.

Sandra's strategy to utterly disregard the shut-up rule and dial her assertiveness way up was an anomaly. If submerging your "feminine side" as the teen did to do well isn't really practical advice, we would still say she was on to something: women who stand up and speak up tend to have a better career and life experience. I've found this to be true, as have so many of the women cited in this book, who've learned to declare what they want and speak their truth. Certainly grown-up Sandra found that to be the case. The popular comedian whose one-woman-shows include *My Boyfriend's Back and There's Gonna Be Laundry* and *Wit's End* didn't become an archeologist, though she says she uses the same tools "to excavate my life" for her material.

If everyone can't enjoy your "unfeminine" behavior, maybe it's just not the end of the world. Relationships expert Jean Hannah Edelstein told the *Daily Mail* that "people expect women to blend into the background—which is, of course, a guaranteed way for them not to advance in their careers. My advice to any woman who feels like she's been judged for talking too much is to keep talking, and to encourage her female colleagues to do so as well—it's the only way that things are going to change."[35]

It's not about being liked

When a former client of ours was appointed to the leadership team of her company, she suddenly felt invisible. She took her place at the table of men, waited for someone to pause for air before inserting her opinion, and watched the discussion continue as if she hadn't spoken. "At first, they just pretended I wasn't there. It was easier for them to keep being the way they were. Even at that level, it's still the high school locker room. Everything's a competition, jockeying for position. Women aren't exposed to the way men are with each other. It's quite the eye-opener."

A lone woman in a sea of men has to work hard to be seen and harder to be heard. She stopped waiting for the pauses. "I started to weigh in on things. That was fun. They don't like a woman challenging them. They think of women as emotional and gushy and they don't want to be around that, but if you're not like that, they don't like you. Talk about being stuck between a rock and a hard place. I don't worry about whether they like me." She arched a brow and said, "I think I raise the tone a bit."

Many shades of gray

If you have any ambition, assertive behavior in the workplace is an absolute must. The way you best express your assertiveness might look a bit different, depending on your company's culture. Ellen Ma, an innovation consultant now based in Singapore, spent five years in a senior marketing role at a national retail giant where "she who speaks loudest and fights hardest wins." It was a career-making role, but the culture was "oil and water" for the collaborative, consensus-building Ellen when she started. She adopted a "when in Rome" mentality; she learned to speak louder and more forcefully, and to roll with others doing the same. Overtly assertive behavior never felt natural to her, and one thing that helped her was the regular support she sought out from women friends; doing things like checking in after especially tough conversations was grounding.

After Ellen left that job and started working in Asia, she learned another tactic for behaving assertively, one that suited her better. Today, Ellen's get-my-way strategy is to float her ideas in a meeting, then work behind the scenes to build support, consensus and buy-in.

I've found that being the one ready to speak first and take the lead works for me; this behavior has generally led to getting my way at every job I've had. Even as a relatively new professional, I saw that declaring a strong preference for an idea or strategy seemed to translate to "Okay, let's do that, then." Susan Cain, the author of *Quiet*, says studies show groups follow the loudest voice in the room (not that they're always right, mind you). Janet benefits from a subtler version of assertive behavior, described in Cain's best-selling book about the 47 percent who are quieter than their loud friends.

Janet puts it this way: "I'm often not the first one to speak in the meeting. I synthesize. I want to know what other people think. I get my power through listening—if you're paying attention, there's a lot of information to use in the conversation. I wait and take in the bigger picture and respond to that, instead of immediately reacting to a piece of the picture. That's how I land my points and get to my goal. My delivery is through intimacy and storytelling."

"Assertive" is many shades of gray, and not just the blunt instrument I favor. Our partnership has worked well because our leadership styles are yin-yang. Janet's approach to asserting a point of view and winning her argument in an important meeting with clients or bosses is often the better fit, and my best strategy is to take a backseat in those situations.

Don't ask, don't get

Are you assertive enough at the job to get what you want and need? Before you answer, ask yourself this: When did you last say no to an unreasonable task at work, like accepting a project you knew you didn't have the time to complete well? When did you last demand what you're worth? The promotion you want? Do you have a pattern of giving a work partner the mic in presentations, maybe feeling a little relieved to let them take the wheel? You can be an extrovert and still fail to behave assertively in situations that demand it. It can all translate to less money, less power, less potential being fulfilled, and unhappiness when you're chronically frustrated.

Executive coach Chris Tardio has seen it many times: women who work hard, hit their goals and assume their efforts will be noticed and rewarded. That's just not how it goes, most of the time. We've said it to so many: if you don't ask, you don't get. Chris has worked with many women who came to executive coaching because they felt stuck in their careers and frustrated after being passed over for promotions. She found that in many cases, the women knew for weeks or sometimes months that a new opportunity was opening up, and they assumed they'd be an obvious choice but never actually raised their hands. "Women need to stand up and be counted," she said. "They've got to ask for what they want."

Take the credit you deserve

Women often fall into the role of team-builder or nurturer of talent. This is a strength, one Janet and I leveraged from the start. But when the desire to be a good "team player" means that we aren't making our individual contribution to projects understood to bosses, clients or the community, the raise, promotion and recognition you're due won't materialize anytime soon.

Hiding your light under a barrel marked "team" isn't nearly as often a problem that guys have. Chris says that men often manage their careers more strategically than women do. Men seem to have more of an inherent or cultivated understanding that if you want to get ahead, you've got to talk yourself up. "Women tend to think that tooting their own horn will make them seem arrogant."

And certainly, some of the research I talked about earlier suggests that women who talk up their achievements don't win points with some of the men around them. But Chris believes that tooting your own horn doesn't have to equate to arrogance if you talk about your accomplishments in a context that's relevant to the conversation at hand.

An unfair advantage

Like Sandra Shamas, I had both nature and nurture setting me up to run with my assertiveness. And like her, it would be years before I actually recognized how that was serving me. I was oblivious to society's strong suggestions to be more, um, demure. I'm pretty sure that as soon as I could talk, I was bossing people around. I also had a role model who demonstrated the benefits of extra-strong every day. My mother, Katharine Taylor Miller, was the daughter of a Southern mom from whom she inherited strength, humor and kindness. She was quick to take a stand, and when she spoke up, she was fearless, no matter whose feathers might be ruffled. If she perceived unfairness in a situation, she would stare down the school principal, the United Way president or our small-town mayor if need be. She was outspoken, bold, smart and headstrong. But I don't think anyone would have labeled her "bossy," perhaps because the package was wrapped so sweetly. Mom had the loudest laugh in the room; she told me that before I could talk, I would imitate her by holding the phone to my ear and laughing. She enjoyed debate so much, she married a man who could ensure it happened daily. Paul Miller, a handsome Yankee from Connecticut, was a Republican. Mother was a Democrat. Very few dinners passed without a loud exchange about the political issue of the day. Picture four children, heads whipping back and forth from one end of the table to the other, over and over. I can't remember a single sentence, just the noise. And yet there was never lingering anger. It was honest enough, fair enough: "We just disagree."

I was incredibly fortunate to be surrounded by strong women as I grew up, Mother's iron-willed friends among them. So I grew up believing that women were meant to be opinionated, loud and confident. I couldn't wait to talk so I could say what I thought (the downside being I suffered from an inability to self-edit. I can remember berating myself as early as the third grade for saying something I knew should have stayed inside my head).

When I entered the workforce, my first boss would further illustrate the benefits of assertiveness. Sam Macuga stands as one of the most self-assured, extroverted women I've ever met. Not any version of perfect, she had a temper that her employees could sense like animals just before an earthquake. "Here she comes—duck." The door would slam open. A bad client meeting. A bad date last night, maybe. Whatever it was, when the Sam storm front moved in, it was a miserable day. Far more often, though, she was a positive force. She explained everything with patience and gave us opportunities to learn daily. She obsessed over details and expected everyone else to. She had high standards, but she wasn't particularly control-freaky. She was okay with giving me lots of rope, knowing I would fail a certain amount of the time. I don't remember being reprimanded for the mistakes that came with learning. Sam's life lessons set me up well, and first and foremost on the list was this: acting confident and speaking up help you command respect and ensure your ideas get noticed. Everything will work out from there.

Assertiveness lessons

You may not have been born with a bullhorn in your hand. Maybe you weren't groomed for assertiveness by a long series of bossy women, either. It took many years before I could look back and attribute my relatively steady rise to these factors, maybe more than any others. Now I see I had an unfair advantage. I'm not really typical. Nor is the less loud Janet, the master of listening. Can an unassertive person even become assertive? Or is that like trying to turn an apple into an orange? For that matter, is it "bad" to be a quieter, more introverted person? Of course not. Half the planet is somewhere on the "introvert" spectrum, and thank goodness every-one isn't walking around at top volume. We think it's just a matter of being mindful of your actions and adopting new habits so you can *behave* more assertively, at work and at home, when that serves you well. Young Sandra's strategy, with a bit more nuance, could help us all. Here you go, at no extra charge: assertiveness lessons.

STEP 1: ACT ASSERTIVE.

Jan Leth, the former global digital creative director of the Ogilvy network, uses an expression I love: "Fake it till you make it." Like magic, if you pretend you're confident, with practice you will become confident. Perception is reality, and from the moment you start wearing a bold face, you will see people respond to you like a leader. Ogilvy Toronto's managing director, Laurie Young, once said to me, "Nance, you're incredible—even when you have no idea what you're talking about, you sound like the expert on the subject." Rather than take that as a know-it-all knock, I'm going to own it as a compliment of sorts. Like Sam before me, I have learned to state a point of view, even if it's not based on absolute certainty. I suspect Sam was faking it a bunch of the time. People who need to be 99 percent sure to speak, won't speak. To all the women who would rather be *sure*, my pitch is go for it. Way more often than not, it's worked for me. If you find later that you got a point wrong, that's where the art of admitting mistakes comes in. (Always own up to being wrong. I'm truly an expert at that.) People have more confidence in you when you put a stake in the ground. Men have known this, well, forever. Many of our clients have told us they won't buy an idea from their agency team if their solid belief in its power isn't coming out of their pores. I can tell you, in advertising, there's no such thing as a sure thing. You can't prove an idea will work. But it's mandatory to behave as if you had supreme confidence.

Many women don't even think about their true desires, because they believe they can't have what they want. They put themselves at the bottom of the list, believing that's how it works, how it should be. The (subconscious) reasoning: you're a dedicated professional, so you look after your health and well-being only if there's any time and energy left for that. If you're a wife and/or parent too, your partner's and children's needs usually trump yours. Friends? Time off? Hobbies? They can start to look like frills. Make time to reflect, to review the big picture? Most don't do that, if it even crosses their minds. But that practice, applied to both personal and professional goals, is a regular feature of happy, successful people.

It's hard to be assertive about what you want when you don't actually know what that is. So, first things first. We use a diabolically simple way to unearth it. The only tools you need are a few sheets of paper and a pen—and a quiet space. The drill is to answer this question, in detail: What would your perfect day look like? From waking to lights out. In every aspect, hour by hour. It's a workday, not a weekend, not a vacation. Here's the trick: you have to consciously blow past all the "but that would never happen" thoughts. Are you single and wishing your ideal mate was part of it? Write down what he looks like, exactly. (Yes, it's okay if he looks just like Brad Pitt.) What's your dynamic? How does he behave? What's his background? Where are you working? What's your role? What's your salary? What are you wearing? What's the trip to work like? What's the important meeting like today, ideally? The lunch? The discussion you scheduled with your boss? Did you or your team come up with a game-changing idea? Did you win an international award for being the first to accomplish something? (No, this doesn't require that you think in terms of Nobel Prize–winning moments; it's about whatever your truest desires are, big or small.) Let your mind go; challenge yourself to let thoughts and images flow. Sound simple? It may take you several sittings to really capture what that day looks like. We become so entrenched in our current realities and the belief that "I can't do that/can't have that," it can be hard to dream.

Now write down what actually happened today, in the same detail. Once you've written it all down, and compared, the hard work begins. The "perfect day" exercise is really about examining the differences between the ideal and the reality, and making a promise to yourself to take steps toward what you really want. The aha moments happen when you challenge all the "I can't" knee-jerk reactions, point by point. Let's say you want a promotion but doubt it will happen. Think about what creates that gap. Perhaps you would say, "The senior slots are taken." Therefore, "I can't" is the conclusion. Then the next question to ask yourself is, "What's the worst that can happen if I tell my boss I want the promotion anyway?" There's no downside to asking for a meeting to discuss your goals—including the title and responsibilities that go with it.

With a thoughtful review of your achievements that illustrate your merits, the worst that can happen is you won't get the promotion. You won't get fired. You won't be branded a troublemaker. In fact, your boss will have a clear picture of your value and ambition thanks to your update and will know that he or she is at risk of losing you if you're not given what you need to be happy. If there's no way to include you in the titled group right now, he owes you a vision of a future that includes you in those ranks—including the projected timing for that. (And if he doesn't think you're there yet, he can identify what you need to do to get there—critical information that your conversation can prompt.) Many women with ambition wait for the boss to recognize and announce that they're ready to lead. The very act of telling him you want the job demonstrates you're a leader. I'll say it again: if you don't ask, you don't get.

Maybe in your perfect day you take a Zumba class every Wednesday at 7:30 a.m. Finally, you've found a badly needed fitness plan you like. In reality, you never take that class because you're expected at work at 9 sharp. Really? What's the worst that could happen if you started arriving at 9:30? Deal breaker? Who would it upset? Perhaps your work partner or closest team member. Think about what could resolve that conflict. Think creatively. Strike a deal where you'll work that much later, or make up for the conference call you missed with a promise to take the next one solo, or whatever your partner might declare is of equal value. Treat the person who may be in a position to mind the change with respect and collaborate on the dilemma.

Once your partner or team member buys in, you can look to your boss for the green light. You'd be amazed at how easily these things can be worked out.

One person we know included her deep desire for a life partner in her perfect day exercise—a wish long suppressed after a failed marriage. A "this will never happen" loop was in her head as she wrote down something most of us want in our lives. But later, she saw that the exercise had prompted her to change behaviors not conducive to meeting someone new, like spending too much time with her good friend, her ex-husband. Conscious changes led to unconscious changes, too. Friends and co-workers noticed that her attitude had became more upbeat. She literally smiled more. Her eating habits became healthier when she didn't need food to feel better. She began wearing more flattering clothes, changing her habit of defaulting to unisex styles, as she took more of an interest in her appearance. Within the year, she was happily involved with a caring man. Professionally she was also standing out more, with greater confidence that came with feeling more authentically herself.

This may sound Pollyanna or like a big, steaming heap of bullshit, but it works. Simply committing to writing down what you really want and reflecting upon every difference between your current reality and your dream reality is incredibly productive. Good things happen when you start shooting holes in the "I can't" list. And it's fast. You may not have the life of your dreams within weeks, but following through with behaviors that align with getting what you want will lead to getting what you want. Sorry that it's so simple. I'd make it complicated if that worked better.

STEP 3: STEP INTO THE SPOTLIGHT. YES, YOU THERE.

It's human to want to sidestep the glare of all eyes on you, and it's a great out if a bolder colleague is eager to take the stage. We've seen it a thousand times. We've done it a thousand times. The most extroverted, confident team member appears in the spotlight again and again at the meetings where the big decisions are made. So often, the partner who made equal or even greater contributions to the work looks on as her colleague makes the case. As leaders, we often bought into the one with the raised hand leading the show. After all, confidence helps to sell the work, and we wanted the odds in our favor. But we got to the point where we performed mini-interventions too. We would take both ham and wallflower aside. The bolder one would be coached on creating space for the part-ner, for the sake of her development, the health of the partnership and, ultimately, better outcomes all around. The one who regularly deferred to her partner would be told she was limiting her career by not getting equal time in front of clients, and she was depriving the group of her insights and opinions. In the worst case, quiet behav-ior leaves an audience with the impression that the reserved partner is "not as smart." They may also think: *She must not have a strong point of view. He must be the real power. I don't know if I have a lot of confidence in her to lead the project. She must be less experienced than him. What's her name again?* Yes, this can be running through heads while you sit there smiling supportively at Joe as he runs the show. Or maybe you're miles from smiling supportively, instead seething with resentment that your more assertive co-worker has elbowed his way to the mic again, or was placed there by your boss. If for some reason you're rarely front and center, it's time to change that.

A common reason people stand in the shadows is pure, simple stage fright. You can suffer from it in front of two thousand people or two, even if you're a big, fat extrovert. We'd say that at least half of the accomplished people in our Swim leadership training are eager to tackle it, and we've seen studies that say over 90 percent of people experience it to varying degrees.

As a child, I jumped at any chance to perform. Rallying parents to come over to my friend Laura's garage for a play was a regular event. I won the lead in my third grade play, happily singing solo in front of hundreds. But by my early teens, as so many girls do, I saw my confidence fade. I avoided any situation where I'd be on a stage. By then, I questioned my talent, and I worried about screwing up. Even after joining a rock band at sixteen and reclaiming some of my enjoyment of performance, when I was given a solo, the terror defeated me. Years later, as a fairly high-profile professional, I said no to judging any awards show where I would be expected to speak, for even a moment, at the ceremony. I pictured passing out, forgetting everything, or hyperventilating. So I just said no, a lot. It was limiting my career. I finally reached a turning point when I got an invitation to chair the prestigious Canadian awards show for the industry's best television advertising. I stared and stared at that piece of paper, willing myself to feel something other than panic and dread as I imagined one thousand of my peers, two thousand eyes. And I said yes. I arrived at that show nine months later, appearing completely relaxed. I now do public speaking with regularity, along with Janet, who also battles stage fright. Here's what I learned: the most effective way to take the edge off the fear is to prepare. (Note: whether you're fearful or not, preparation is still your best shot at persuading anyone to buy what you're selling.) And do it often. The more you go ahead and perform, the less scary it becomes.

Here's some simple advice on how to prepare for that speech or the opening to the big meeting, which will help you to appear confident and natural. Step one is to capture your story. There are many, many good ways to do this, but mine is to write it out spontaneously in longhand. Don't overthink. When you're finished, think more about your best story arc. What's your strongest possible first sentence, one that will make everybody want to listen? What's your strongest possible closing line, one they'll still remember later that night? What's the climax of your story? Once you identify these three key elements, it's fairly easy to nail your story. Read the whole rewrite out loud a couple of times. You'll hear what doesn't quite work and what's extraneous. Now boil your story down to bullet points, just a few words per thought. Rehearse, using these brief notes as your rails.

It's perfectly fine to use notes when you speak. I admire the Bill Clintons of the world, who seem able to stay on point no matter how much ground they have to cover. But for the rest of us, there's no need to feel awkward about looking down to see your next point. What may seem like an eternity to you looks like a thoughtful pause to the audience. Odd, but true. You know what people do think is lame? Winging it and then going off on tangents, thoughts all over the place. Notes that keep you on point, calm and relaxed are priceless. If you rehearse privately several times before your meeting or event, your brain will do a lot of work for you. You may well find you don't need your notes much in the meeting or on the stage. You will be subconsciously drawing on the process and it will dissolve most of your fear. If you make a mistake, who really cares? It endears you to your audience that you're human. Janet has people paying close attention thanks to her habit of drawing on whatever happened on the way to the meeting. She finds that entering the room as a human being first lowers the tension, and even the most senior group follows her lead. Better things happen in a more informal room; when everyone's guard comes down, better dialogue is possible. Breaking the ice this way calms her nerves too.

For those who can access it, we highly recommend another route to putting yourself out there confidently. Take an acting or improv class. Both Janet and I have done this, years apart. We both went to New York for a weekend actor's workshop that includes non-actors, run by a great acting coach, Deena Levy. She puts a group of twelve through a series of vocal exercises, physical exercises, improv and scene reading. I was glad I didn't realize before I went that improv would be part of it; I wouldn't have had the guts to go. The course was designed to positively reframe taking chances and risking looking foolish. We were expected to give 100 percent to every exercise, no matter how uncomfortable that might be. By late afternoon Sunday, all the students felt as though we'd been through the war together and were happy for having proven to ourselves that we could perform, often quite well, under really challenging conditions. We found our inner child, hidden under layers of armor put on every day to cope with the emotionally challenging parts of our jobs. Everyone found that in letting go of our self-consciousness, an inner joy had come bounding out. For the woman who had told the inner girl many years ago that she couldn't act, shouldn't perform, it was a great, giddy shock to find improv exhilarating. I had new-found confidence in putting my thoughts forward boldly, and the bonus was a big dent in stage fright. The famous Second City, and many other improv and theater troupes, offer workshops that have similar benefits.

We've also had traditional training in presentation skills, which was very helpful. But the acting and improv route works at another level; I'd say it helps students get comfortable being themselves in any setting. The real you is not a mute. We've seen shy people emerge from improv able to own the room. It's a way to up your game and move past "performance" as an experience to be avoided. Once you've unleashed yourself, there's no going back—not even for the most introverted. Especially after you've seen how positive the reaction is from all around you.

Amy Cuddy is a social psychologist who studies nonverbal behavior—particularly body language. She suggests a great exercise that's especially good for all of us who are nowhere near dying for our turn on the stage. She notes that before any high-stress meeting or situation, like a speech, you can be far better poised to project confidence and have more presence by "power posing" before walking into the spotlight. By finding a private moment to literally strike the Wonder Woman pose (hands on hips, legs apart), or the pose of the runner who just crossed the finish line (arms up, head back, huge grin), you will release testosterone and lower cortisol, which will make you feel calmer and more confident. Smiling, that simple act, triggers good chemistry. Amy says, "Our bodies change our minds and our minds change our behavior. And our behaviors change our outcomes." She tells us, don't fake it till you make it; fake it till you *become* it.

One more trick to doing your best when the pressure's on comes through cognitive scientist Sian Beilock. Her studies find you can train your brain to perform your best under pressure, and essentially avoid the big choke so many of us dread. Under great stress, the emotional centers of the brain become overactive, preventing clear thinking. We've all seen people choke, and we've done it our-selves, stumbling on the test, the speech or the big presentation. As she explains it, it's as if there's way too much chatter between the prefrontal cortex and the emotional centers of the brain. The people who don't experience stress under pressure are managing to keep that exchange from happening. Beilock found an unbelievably simple way to replicate the brain activity of the non-stressed sub-jects she worked with. When people spent ten minutes journaling before high-stress events, writing down their deepest fears about the upcoming event and concluding with what they wanted to happen—basically, to relax—their brain function improved signifi-cantly and they were able to perform their best. This highly accom-plished scientist who had her Olympic soccer dream destroyed when she choked as a teen says she journals now before her high-stress events.[36] I'm using ten little minutes before my next big meeting to write and to strike the Wonder Woman pose. Hopefully, there won't be any hidden cameras in the room.

There. Three not-totally easy steps to being a force to be reck-oned with. For the people who may wonder what's come over you, for the few who may prefer a more demure you, know this truth about humans: most people respond positively to confidence and conviction. When you step up and put your great ideas and thoughts forward fearlessly, you will be on your way to making a greater impact that's good for you and the team around you. Your career will naturally advance. You can be sure it will take a lot longer to achieve goals when you aren't seen and heard.

Lose the fear and ignore the "keep it down" signals that may linger. Get in touch with the bossypants deep inside and let her take you far.

RULE TO BE BROKEN:

Because you're not worth it.

In my second ad agency job, after my three-month hiccup writing "women's striped cotton top with pale blue piping and 3-button placket" for the Sears catalogue, my boss would occasionally swing by my office to let me know I'd see "a little extra" on my paycheck. This went on for two years. I found the idea of asking for money terrifying, so I was giddy with relief when that sensitive man spared me all the awkwardness and humiliation. When you're earning fourteen thousand dollars a year, even a few hundred dollars feels like a fortune, so it never occurred to me that his generosity added up to less than twenty dollars a week. In my world, it was always Christmas. Then my slightly older writer friend, who lived by the motto, "when you're a small, young woman, you need to be a big bitch to be taken seriously," dragged me into her office for a "big talk." The subject? My salary. She wanted to know how much I earned. My back went up. Everyone knows you don't talk about money.

"What's it to you?" I asked her. Gracious.

"Well, you spend an awful lot of time whining about how broke you are," she said. "Maybe I can give you some perspective." She had a point. I whispered my sad little number.

She shook her head at me. "You do know you're getting hosed, right? By letting him come to you, you're taking the smallest amount he can get away with. Not only that, you're grateful. How dumb can you be?" She pulled a little book out of her drawer. It was a log of her accomplishments, her bargaining chips.

Our agency had had a jackpot year. She wanted to know what role I'd played in that. I'd played a role? Not as far as I could tell. But lo and behold, when we went through it all, my regular contributions began to leap out. "Write it down, then go tell him what you want and why you should get it." I thanked her for her advice. Then, as we parted ways, she left me with this: "Grow up, little girl."

I booked a meeting, and knocked on the boss's door, clutching my notes, feeling as guilty as a kid with a bad report card. Somehow, I got the ask out. He seemed surprised. Hadn't he just given me a raise? Hadn't he always been good to me? Considerate?

I could hear my mother's voice saying, "Don't brag," but I mumbled out my list before I lost my nerve. "I helped on three pitches and we won them all; I got a radio award and sold four campaigns, not by myself, of course." I spoke while looking down at my paper. Silence. I looked up. I could see the light going on. He didn't really know what I did, which ideas were mine, which tough clients I had good relationships with. On a regular day, I'd rather have died than told him, but I was eight months pregnant, living on a shoestring, and very motivated. He agreed that I should earn more.

Woo-hoo! I'd be coming back from maternity leave to a five-thousand-dollar raise. Whew. The raise-to-be was quickly converted into a crib, a stroller, a bassinet, a tower of diapers, drawers full of onesies. So what if we went into debt buying all that stuff? The money was on its way, and babies go through a lot of diapers.

Four months later, I went back to work expecting a shiny, bigger paycheck to plug the hole in my bank account, only to find that my boss had left for another agency without putting through my raise. Cue the opening notes of Beethoven's Fifth. *Duh, duh, duh, daaa.* The agency refused to honor the commitment with only my word to go on. *Duh, duh, duh, daaa.* So there I was with a colicky new baby, an equally broke young husband, and a mortgage that kept us in the poorhouse. I was stunned. Furious, resentful and hurt, I stuck around, afraid to quit, hoping something would change. I nervously scanned the job scene.

"I hear you're looking for work." My ex-boss was on the phone. *You'll betray me again,* I thought. Does "betray" seem like a strong word to you? Maybe it was just that he was careless, but I didn't want to work for him again. Good girl to the last, I agreed to meet.

I was up to a whopping sixteen thousand a year and figured I'd really raise the stakes if it looked as if he wanted to bring me in.

"Twenty-five thousand," I said, all tough.

He looked surprised. "Then I must give you five thousand more than that."

Was he crazy? Did I say, "Why, thank you. That's very generous. Let me sleep on it and get back to you"? Did I say, "Yahoo!" and fling my hat in the air? I did not. I said, ". . . but I'm not worth that." I actually said those words.

"You should always be worth more to me than you are to you," he replied. I took the job on the spot.

Who's the worthiest of them all?

When you go from fourteen thousand to sixteen thousand dollars over two years, and suddenly to thirty thousand over the course of half an hour, it doesn't compute. I simply couldn't believe I deserved twice as much tomorrow for doing the same job as I did today but in a different company. I didn't have any clear idea of what the job was worth, but I was sure it wasn't that high—which is a typical way to think even now for young women. Branding firm Universum does an annual survey of undergrads and MBA students, asking them to anticipate what their starting salaries will be. As recently as 2012, women students guessed roughly seven thousand dollars less than the guys did.[37] Even when we're guessing, when the sky is still the limit, we under-reach.

When I was a teenager, you got your after-school or summer job through the help-wanted ads in the local newspaper. The listings were laid out in columns with "Help Wanted: Male" and "Help Wanted: Female" across the top. I never looked at the male column for obvious reasons, but if I'd been on the job hunt ten years earlier, I might have noticed that some of the very same jobs appeared in both columns, with a lower salary for women.[38]

A few decades later, things haven't changed as much as you'd expect. The latest figures from the U.S. government show that women now earn about three-quarters of what men earn—seventy-seven cents for every dollar pocketed by men. It's true in law, teaching, engineering. The Institute for Women's Policy Research has predicted that the wage gap between men and women won't close until 2056. Others say it may be ninety-eight years before women's pay catches up to men's.

I'm not keen on waiting an entire century for wage parity, and I fear the continuing snail's pace when I read studies like the one from the National Academy of Sciences that shows the identical made-up résumé gets different results if a woman's name is at the top, rather than a man's. Corinne Moss-Racusin and other Yale researchers found that chemistry and physics profs saw John as more competent and worthy of a job and mentoring and deserving of a higher salary than Jennifer.[39] Similar studies have been conducted with students at Stanford Graduate School of Business, based on the Harvard Business School case cited by Sheryl Sandberg in *Lean*

In: half the students were asked to go online and rate the entrepreneur Heidi (Heidi Roizen is a real person), and the other half to rate Howard (Howard is not a real person) based on the same résumé, and qualifications. Once again, the woman, Heidi, took a huge hit in comparison to Howard. Students didn't like her, used words like "power-hungry" and "self-promoting," and didn't want to work with her.[40] Bias starts young and it means that in business, Keith is the guy they want to hang out with, who'll get the job done and who deserves the glittering paycheck. As for Kate? She really doesn't seem as qualified, does she? She probably won't be a great employee, so she should earn less than Keith, especially if she's a mom. What did Kate ever do to them?

A cartoon from *The Christian Science Monitor* captures it perfectly: A woman in an office is reading a newspaper with the headline "Gender Gap in Wages." The man beside her is looking at her and saying, "Three-quarters of a penny for your thoughts." Nailed. It would be funny if it weren't so sad.

The mountain of articles and research papers and panel discussions on why women are less financially successful than men could fill the Treasury. The arch villain here is the unconscious bias grandfathered into a system that was created by men for men at a time when most women stayed home with their kids. The research points to our long history of being "second salaries" or working for "pin money." Our history of part-time work has cast us in supporting roles, as has our tendency to go into "helping professions" like nursing and teaching, jobs that focus on people rather than wealth creation, jobs that our society cares about less.

Explanations are good, but they don't change a darn thing. And the system is in no hurry to change itself, which means it's up to us. At the very least, each one of us can ask for what she wants. Sylvie, the very senior in-house counsel for a heavy machinery manufacturing company, and my seatmate on a flight to Chicago, didn't agree. She'd given up her fancy partner-track job in a corporate law firm because it was killing her teenage son to have two "sure-I'll-be-at-your-football-game-sorry-I-can't-make-it" parents. She knew it meant less money, but a couple of years in, she'd become incredibly disillusioned with the workload-paycheck trade. When I suggested she build a case for more, she gave me the "you don't get it" face. She'd completely bought into the belief that she couldn't change things.

Good girls don't arm-wrestle, but it's time to learn

"I've never negotiated a salary in my life." Judith Wright, the former deputy minister of Children and Youth Services for the Ontario government, a department of five thousand people, shook her head in disbelief at her own complicity in the don't-ask-don't-get experience of so many women. "Not as assistant deputy of health or environment. Not as the deputy of health promotion and sport, Pan Am Games or intergovernmental affairs. What was I thinking?" The public service was a calling, like the priesthood, and she believed that you should just be happy with what you got. Did men buy into that? Of course not. After she left her post, her replacement told his bosses that he was bringing them important new contacts from the private sector. He told them an impressive story. Then he took on half her old job and negotiated a salary $150,000 higher. He asked; he got.

I'm far from the only woman who has felt she wasn't worth more money. What a club to be part of. Senior legal counsel, deputy minister, chief creative officer—we all have fancy titles, and years of accomplishment, and still, for many of us, the idea of asking for money is right up there with sticking pins in our eyes . . . and for the most part, we have the paychecks to prove it.

Deborah Meek of WorkHarmony, a Toronto recruiting firm, was excited about Anika's chances of landing a terrific job at a large marketing company. The MBA grad had been interviewed several times, with ever-more influential people. Anika approached each meeting with the focus and detail orientation of a forensics expert. "You know I'm nailing this," she said. Deb did know. It was the fifth interview, ostensibly the final one, and if bookies had been laying odds, Anika was the odds-on favorite.

"We're agreed that you're going to ask for $65K, right?" They'd been debating the number for weeks, Deb recommending, Anika countering with less as Deb attempted to stretch Anika's comfort zone. Deb raising, Anika lowering.

Raising. Lowering. It was typical behavior for a woman and intensely frustrating for Deborah, who finds women easier to place than men. "They're more confident, more poised. They speak better. They're perceptive. They've got it all going on, except where money is concerned." The problem? She can never convince women to ask for what they're worth.

"Men are better poker players," she said. "They insinuate they'll walk away if they don't get what they want. They understand the bluff: start high and come down if necessary. Women ask for less to begin with, almost never push back on an offer, and then use the fact that they've undersold themselves as a stick to beat themselves with. And those patterns stick."

How sad that we've been stuck in molasses for the entire decade since Linda Babcock and Sara Laschever's much-quoted 2003 study showing that 57 percent of young men negotiate their first salary, while only 7 percent of women do. Let that sink in for a minute. Fifty-seven percent of guys negotiate their first salary. Gutsy or what? I'd no more have negotiated my first salary than sprouted gold-encrusted wings. A more recent look at starting salaries for grads by Rutgers's John J. Heldrich Center for Workforce Development confirms that young women are taking home over five thousand dollars less than young men. And in Canada, the most recent numbers are considerably worse. Young women MBAs are earning about eight thousand dollars less than men in their first post-MBA jobs.[41]

Professor Beatrix Dart from the Rotman School of Management agrees that young women do better in school, interview better, get hired just as often, yet come out on the low end of salary negotiation at the beginning and stall out as they gain seniority. "When I ask them why, they say that's what they were offered. 'Did you counter?' The answer is always the same: 'I was too uncomfortable.'"

Our lack of confidence shows up in various disguises: silence, acceptance—and it shows itself in our pay. Professor Dart calls it "note-taker syndrome." She always asks who took the notes when her students are working on a project in groups. Would you be shocked if I told you the "secretary" is usually a woman? Stand up and lead the discussion. "Start sitting back, stay sitting back" is the rule, she tells them. "So get up there. You paid just as much for your degree as the men."

So what does this mean in the long run? According to *Fast Company*, it means a half million dollars that we're throwing over our shoulders like a bride's bouquet.[42] The mistake is that we don't negotiate our salaries when we're young. We start behind and stay behind, at least in part, by our own hand. If this sounds a bit like blaming the victim, well, I am the victim, and I certainly blame myself.

I'll say it again using a different source this time: SOME EXPERTS HAVE SUGGESTED WOMEN LOSE BET- WEEN $350,000 AND $500,000 IN SALARY BECAUSE WE DON'T START TO NEGOTIATE UNTIL WE'RE TOO FAR BEHIND TO CATCH UP.[43] The caps are intentional; I'm shout- ing here. Why doesn't anyone tell us this? Would knowing this long ago have changed the way I handled myself early in my career? Will hearing it change what you do? I hope so.

Male nurses can take in up to ten thousand dollars more a year than female nurses.[44] Male physician-researchers earn over twelve thousand dollars per year more than their women counterparts. Do the math and weep. Over a thirty-five-year career, this discrepancy can cost women $465,000 in lost earnings.[45] Even in partnership organizations like accounting or legal firms, women partners can find themselves taking home over 40 percent less than the men,[46] according to She Negotiates partner Lisa Gates. Imagine how many more years you'd have to work to make it up.

Which is why it's heartening to hear Lisa Gates say that this isn't the end of the story. "Women don't have to keep losing money. While they're not going recapture the money left on the table over the years, women can still capture the top of their current market value. If closing the gap between today's paycheck and true market value would make your employer's eyes spin in circles, negotiate timing for getting to parity. We should never say, 'Oh well. Too late. I missed the parity boat,'" Lisa advises. "Getting past the gravitational pull of one's existing salary is the hard part." This is no time to be fine with the status quo.

Let the broad do it

"Will nothing ever change?" Claire Lamont was seething. One of Vancouver's Top 40 Under 40 entrepreneurs by the time she was twenty-nine, Claire was in a fury as she sipped her Old Maid (gin, cucumber, mint, lime and Demerara sugar—I know you wanted to know) and told us about a women's networking event she'd attended the previous week. The audience was glued to a conversation between two longtime journalists.

The bad old days of women in the newsroom came up. One of the speakers recalled an incident from her past where there was a human interest piece looking for someone to write it. The editor, barely looking up from his desk, said, "Let the broad do it."

"Is this still the case?" someone in the audience wanted to know.

The other speaker told the room that journalism had changed a great deal since those days, that, in fact, it's become a woman' s business, in the field, in the anchor's or co-anchor's seat. She suggested that they're actually struggling to find men to step into journalistic roles.

"And then she said very casually," Claire's face was pink with anger, her South African accent even more clipped as the words flew out of her mouth. "'I guess we'll have to raise wages to recruit more men.' What? Did I hear her right? I waited for her to say, 'Just kidding,' and then we'd all laugh together. But she didn't."

Claire scribbled the comment on the sheet in front of her.

"The talk ended and they started passing the mic around for questions. I waited for the firestorm, but no one said anything. It was as if they hadn't noticed. It was all work-life balance and what's it like to be a war correspondent."

The woman sitting next to Claire was practically jumping out of her seat as she said, "Ask your question, ask your question." She'd heard it too.

Claire put up her hand and repeated back to the journalist what she'd said almost word for word. "You said the industry has come a long way based on how many more women there are, but you also said that you'd have to increase wages if you want to recruit more men. Isn't that just another way of saying, 'Let the broad do it'?"

Silence.

The journalist told Claire that she must have misunderstood. Of course men would never be paid more than women.

"But you did say you'd have to pay more to bring in men. Why don't you just pay women better?" Claire was a dog with a bone.

Just a few days after hearing Claire's story, I had dinner with two journalist friends who confirmed that the demographics of journalism really are changing—it's becoming a woman's game, largely because men don't feel it pays enough.

Our lower self-esteem, our discomfort with merchandising our achievements, the sense that, at its heart, money is bad and that women, in particular, shouldn't talk about it goes directly to our bottom line. Lisa Jacobson, CEO of Inspirica, a New York–based tutoring company, once told *The Wall Street Journal* that in the twenty years since she'd founded her company, none of the female professionals she hired had ever quoted as high a fee as their male counterparts. "The women almost always say, 'I'm $125 an hour, but for you I'd charge \$75, when the guy just says flatly that he charges \$350," she said.[47]

Amanda Steinberg, the founder and CEO of DailyWorth, a rocket of a women's financial website, gets steaming mad just thinking about pay inequity. "I have to simmer myself down," she said as we started to talk. "Part of why I started my business was because I noticed patterns around me. A friend who is the executive director of a large nonprofit had barely negotiated enough salary to cover her rent. And another one who was doing major marketing strategy projects for Fortune 500 companies was afraid to send invoices, because she wasn't sure if her work was good enough. Sooo frustrating. That was four years ago and I still see it happen every day. 'Am I doing a good enough job?' 'Why should they listen to me?' 'Do you think I'm asking for too much?' And on and on. Women won't truly move forward until we get over ourselves and take control of our financial lives." According to Amanda, Sylvie and I, Deputy Wright and maybe you are paid less, in part, because we act as if were worth less.

So—why? What's underneath all that discomfort? Amanda thinks it goes way back, to the cradle, where the fairy tales teach us we'll be rescued by princes. Most of us are raised with the idea that talking about money isn't polite and that focusing on it is wrong, that if we do, we're greedy or selfish, both of which are bad, hence money is bad. So we surrender our financial lives to our fathers, husbands, brokers, financial planners or any knight with a white horse. We'll do anything not to be involved with it, but handing over the responsibility doesn't relieve us of the anxiety. Becoming a bag lady is one of women's greatest fears, even when they earn over $200,000.[48] Amanda observes that men see money as something to be gained, whereas women see it as something to be lost. It's the price we pay for giving up control and accepting the status quo.

Nancy and I believe it's high time we all did something about it. We did, but we learned the hard way, the seriously underpaid way.

Happy to be here isn't enough

You know how people say, "My job is so great, I can't believe I get paid to do it." In the mid-1990s, Nancy and I were those people. We were best friends sitting around and coming up with ideas just like on TV. We had the best gig in advertising and we made the most of it. We were on a roll: our awards literally toppled a table. We helped turn Ogilvy into the place where everyone wanted to work, but it never occurred to us to parlay that into a golden egg.

The job offers started to come from within Canada, the United States and the United Kingdom. We kept turning them down without thinking twice. Who'd want to leave the best job in the world?

Then we noticed something curious in those job offers: a lot more money. We called up friends in other agencies and phoned headhunters and asked if this was happening because we were the flavor of the moment or because we had been hideously underpaid for way too long. I still see us sitting together in my office, black couch, red wall. We hung up the phone and looked at each other, silent—an extremely rare event. Our eyes were wide as it sank in: definitely and spectacularly underpaid. I remember feeling incredibly stupid and a bit angry. No one takes advantage of you without your permission. It was time to take it back.

One of the offers on the table was from another big agency for double the money. *Double*. We scripted the talk with our CEO. We worked it through from every angle. We rehearsed, sometimes with Nancy playing his role, sometimes with me, until we felt that we couldn't be blindsided or sweet-talked into less than what we wanted. Then we walked down the hall.

He leaned back in his chair, tapped a loafered foot against the side of his desk and let us know he thought we were holding up the bank. "This is the most the network is willing to pay," he said, putting a new number on the table. It wasn't enough, we insisted. We wanted what the industry was willing to pay, and by the way, we had another offer and the clock was ticking. He matched it. For the second time in my life, sucking it up and deciding to go for it put helium in my salary.

What changed? We hadn't magically become super-negotiators. But we had given ourselves a smack upside the head, and a faux "negotiation for dummies" course. It took research, planning, practice, asking, brinkmanship, nail-biting. But none of it was as hard as looking at ourselves in the mirror and recognizing this: however well we did our jobs, as long as we were willing to quietly and gratefully receive what was given to us, we were leaving our careers in the hands of others. We didn't actually want to leave Ogilvy at that time, but we would have. Our crash course in negotiating had taught us that important rule: if you're going to use another offer as leverage, you need to be prepared to follow through.

We had to figure out how to be our own advocates and move beyond the queasiness that goes with being seen to chest beat. Money goes where employers perceive the value. I once had a boss say, "We not only need to be valuable to our clients. We need to be *seen* to be valuable to our clients." I'd thought that was a cynical statement and promptly fell headfirst into the trap of being the woman who believed that if you did a great job, people would see it and shower you with praise and big bucks. I had a rude awakening. Men have no difficulty making sure they are seen as valuable. Men have no trouble making sure they're seen. Period. We wait for someone to notice and then feel hard done by if they don't.

We say, forget feeling hard done by; test-drive asking for what you want and deserve. You may be surprised by how often things go your way. In 2010, a friend of ours was asked to open a new branch of the company she worked for. *Look at me, I'm an entrepreneur*, she told herself. Over a couple of years, her little 'start-up' grew, but her paycheck didn't. Money from her office flowed into the parent company. She put up her hand. A big bonus was in the cards, they said. A year passed. They hedged. She'd had enough already; she broke down the story so they could see how the success tracked back to her initiatives and ideas. "I need you to understand what I've done, how I did it, and be clear that I'm not going to be able to keep doing it if things can't change," she told her bosses. "I love this company. I've been here a long time, but it would be a good idea if this company showed that it loves me." It wasn't personal. No weapons were drawn. She was just stating facts. Within weeks, the Brinks truck backed up to her door.

Our friend wrestled the money monster to the ground with grace, confidence and stylish heels dug in. Here are some things to think about when you're in her shoes.

TELL A BETTER TALE.

Women don't always tell their stories well or even at all. We worry that we'll be seen as that lowest of all creatures: a self-promoter. Even the word makes us squirm. So we either don't knock on our bosses' doors, letting them think we're just fine with the status quo, or we ask for what we want without helping them understand why we should get it. Which is odd when you think that storytelling is women's natural medium. How many of our conversations start with "You won't believe what happened today," or "Call me. I've got the best story to tell you." Painting verbal pictures is how we talk about our lives to our friends, lament a relationship disaster to our mothers, it's how we bring our workday home to our partners.

When I took my list to my boss's office, the story I told didn't mesh with his perception of me. That little jolt gave him a reason to see me with blinders off. I wasn't merely the young bottom-feeder who did all the jobs no one else wanted. I was a teeny-weeny playaah. But it wasn't real even to me until I started to write it down. That scribbled list was a big eye-opener for me. Even so, I don't imagine I'd have gone to him if I hadn't been driven by my baby-to-be and a kick in the pants from my co-worker.

The story makes the difference. We know people in organizations with salary freezes who accept those freezes and haven't had pay increases in five years, while others in the same companies with the same pay freezes have managed to negotiate increases despite the kryptonite lock on the corporate wallet, thanks to more vivid storytelling.

BUT WHAT IF THEY SAY NO?

It can happen and we take "no" personally; the little girl who got left off the birthday party list, was told that nice girls don't ask for things or that boys don't like girls who are pushy is never far from the surface. Instead of debating, we tend to accept the "no" grudgingly, feeling resentful and angry and turned off our company. It's what I did when my boss left without passing on my raise request and then the organization wouldn't honor it. Most men, on the other hand, go straight to "Well, how can I change that? What can I do to turn this no into a yes?"

Alan Webber talks about "taking 'no' as a question" in his terrific book on leadership, *Rules of Thumb*. The insightful co-founder of

Fast Company rightly points out that "yes" isn't always the right answer from the boss. You may assume you're due the money because you've put in the time, stayed late, been a good team player, but what if that isn't what they're looking for? What if they want to see a radical new approach to finding talent, or a new business win as a result of your efforts, or an extraordinary client relationship that hikes your value? How are you measuring up to the company's goals? What could you be doing instead? Just asking the question "what does success look like?" can let your boss know you're on the right track to earning the increase.

Our friend tied her case directly to what the company had asked of her, and she was crystal clear about what she wanted. Many of us aren't. We saw it when we were on the giving-money-out side of the equation, and it wasn't just about raises. When we were hiring, most men came in with a figure in mind, while most women would say, "Well, this is what I'm making now."

When women did ask for actual dollars, they didn't always base it in reality. We were looking at a super-talented mid-level writer–art director team. We knew the woman well. She was clever, gifted and a joy to have around, and her new partner had an excellent reputation. When the time came to discuss money, they asked to do it separately. The young woman asked for fifty thousand dollars more than her partner. I'm sorry—what was she thinking? What made her worth so much more than him? She didn't know. She only knew that one of her former classmates was earning an astronomical salary and believed she should be too. Clearly, she'd learned the "ask for what you want" lesson without the "how to make a case for why you deserve it" part. She hadn't taken into consideration the level of achievement of her classmate. He'd won major awards and had a heap of fame to his name, which gave him a huge upper hand. She was talented but didn't yet have the accomplishments to command the same kind of number.

WHAT IF THEY DON'T LIKE ME?

Fuggedaboudit. There's an uncomfortable paradox in needing to be clear about what you want without being perceived as demanding. Just thinking about it gives me a brain cramp. You have to put aside your "good girl" issues. Good girls don't ask for things, and you need to. The reviews on how women should ask are mixed. While recruiters and professors and HR directors are pointing out that women get further and richer when they ask for what they want, Harvard associate professor Hannah Riley Bowles's 2010 study showed that when women are very direct in their ask, they not only don't always get, they can actively hurt their own reputations, because men don't like women who are too in-your-face. It's a horrible conundrum. What are we to make of this? What line should we walk? Most of us find it challenging to ask for more money, but it's less hard for us to ask for something that is for the good of the group. Bowles suggests framing up your request in how your efforts help the company; this gives perspective to the conversation, which can make all the difference.[49] Everything is immeasurably more complex for women in the business world, and money is the most sensitive subject. It's how we understand our value: to avoid asking for it leaves us feeling as if we don't matter. Asking for it puts us in danger of being seen as all the things we fear: boastful, demanding, overreaching. Nevertheless, even with all the potential peril, we say go for it. This isn't about being liked. It's about self-respect and fairness.

HOW DO YOU LEARN TO NEGOTIATE? PRACTICE ON WORLD PEACE. It's a lot easier to negotiate on behalf of others than it is on behalf of yourself. When Nancy and I went to bat for raises for our people, we did our best to make the case open and shut. Who wouldn't want to give them more after hearing about the knotty problems they'd solved so cleverly, the clients who'd have trusted them with their firstborn? Not convinced? We had another arrow in the quiver. And another. We negotiated with our account people, our clients, our producers and our boss. There was so much negotiation involved in our every day that we joked we should work at the U.N.

Maybe it's worth having someone else tell you your own story while you take notes. Or go to guy school. My husband was always negotiating—bargaining—in markets and stores, abroad and at home. When I went with my cousin's boyfriend, Rob, to buy shoes at Bloomingdale's, he talked the salesman into a 10 percent discount on the already discounted price. At Bloomingdale's. Who does that? Men, that's who. I was dying a thousand deaths. He was right at home. How do you know unless you ask? He took the salesman's card, thanked him profusely and said he'd write a recommendation to his boss. The art of negotiation is a delicate one. To do it well, everyone has to win. The exchange should feel fair. If you can help your employer not just see but feel your value to them, they win and so will you.

V IS FOR VICTORY.

Though never an Oscar-winning bank account builder, I improved over time. That doesn't mean you can't do it better a whole lot sooner. Think about the trick Nancy mentioned a few pages ago, recommended by social psychologist Amy Cuddy: two minutes in front of the bathroom mirror, throwing your arms up into the "victory" stance, before you go in to make your case will send your odds of succeeding waaay up. If ever there was a moment to look just a little nuts to the woman following you into the "Ladies," this is it.

WE HAVE WAYS OF MAKING YOU TALK.

Most organizations hate when their employees discuss salary. It's not unusual to hear your boss say things like, "I'm going to give you a bonus (or raise or take your team out for dinner) but please don't discuss it with anyone else." I'm not proud to say that I've complied with this request. Maybe you have too, but silence implies consent. Not talking about it is good for the company, but it does a big, fat lot of nothing for you. If you don't talk about what you earn, it's extremely hard to know when you're being paid fairly and when you're being taken for a ride. Lilly Ledbetter, the woman at the center of the Fair Pay Restoration Act, the first bill signed into law by Barack Obama, found her male counterparts' salaries anonymously scribbled onto her pay envelope. If someone hadn't nosed into my early salary, I would've never known that I was terrifically underpaid. That conversation was the gift that kept on giving. Most of us aren't as lucky. So we have to sniff out the information, like anteaters seeking, umm, ants. Ask your colleagues (and not just the women), your friends in similar jobs, headhunters, and look on the web. Yes, even go to job interviews. Understanding the objective value of the job you do is the key to being paid properly. This is one of the real places where knowledge equals power.

I was blown away by the story of Ann Price, who left General Electric after a salary dispute—her male employee earned more than her—and started her own software firm where she made all the salaries transparent to every employee. She described each job and set of responsibilities, including her own, and explained why each position was worth the money it got. If people wanted to earn more, they had a clear idea of what they needed to do to get it.[50]

OF COURSE, THERE'S MORE TO THE STORY THAN MONEY.
When Nancy and I decided to take the chief creative officer role as a team, we agreed to lower starting salaries than creative directors

would normally earn, because "after all, there's only a budget for one person in the role." Men might not have accepted that quite so readily. They might have counteroffered, bluffed, and walked away if they weren't satisfied. But we looked at the fact that there's more to job happiness than money. We had a great partnership we wanted to continue in, worked in a place we cared about, and wanted to be as hands-on as possible in raising our kids—doing the job together would make that viable. Our bank accounts would be fatter today if we'd changed agencies, accepted jobs in another country or, duh, demanded more from the get-go. But staying paid off in countless ways, and our advice is unwavering: the money matters, but so do many other factors as you chart your course.

DANGER, WILL ROBINSON.

There's one time when going for the biggest payday is genuinely the wrong thing to do, and that's when money is the only, or even the main, reason to take a job. There are people who believe they're worth whatever they can get. We've seen a lot of careers nosedive that way. The wrong job for big bucks is a formula for regret. We know a clever young team that was doing smart, award-winning work. The writer had a year more experience than the art director, who was straight out of school. They'd started having the "who earns what" chat. She thought it was unfair that he earned more than she did. They were working on the same stuff, getting the same attention, but his experience meant he was better with clients, had greater understanding of the issues that cropped up. He needed less hand-holding: that made him worth more at that stage of his career. She didn't buy it, and soon they left together for a jump in pay at an agency with less opportunity. They lost their momentum for a few dollars and an ego stroke. Taking a job for money may buy you a nicer holiday or a swankier car, but it's still a job you took for the wrong reasons, and that can hold back or even kill a career.

What is what I do worth? How do I put a value on my contribution? Financial guru Amanda Steinberg has a wish: "I want women to hold their own economic and financial prosperity on a par with their contributions in the world and see them as interconnected." What invaluable advice. Here are our final thoughts on this, our most hated subject: do the homework, write the script, practice it over and over, put on your big girl pants and ask for what you want.

I'll do it myself, thanks.

"I think you could use some support." When Daryl Dickinson said these words to a frazzled-looking Janet one afternoon a couple of years into her copywriting career, he may as well have slapped her face. She went red—and saw red—at the suggestion she wasn't up to doing the writing on her massive financial account project by herself. Even though it was obvious to the well-meaning account director (and maybe, deep down, to her too) that more hands would be appropriate, she preferred to risk failure. Over a few hellish weeks, Janet worked insane hours to get the project done. Ultimately she pulled it off, but she learned the hard way that she'd made a mistake. Putting every other project and obligation on hold—including an important, long-planned family event—led to a slew of negative fallout. She lived to regret her dug-in heels and swore she'd never snub her nose at an offer of badly needed help again.

We've seen women refuse to seek help when they're in over their heads again and again. Like the young Janet, they perceive that asking for help smacks of "weaker sex." So they suck it up. The problem is that this puts them at risk of facing consequences of all sorts when outcomes are bad. In spite of coaching our employees to declare limits when they were overextended, Janet and I lived through countless problems that came directly from the stoic, horribly misguided "I can do it myself" mantra.

Don't commit yes-icide

One frantic Monday morning, I had an urgent project put in front of me by an account director who was sweating bullets. Our fast-food client wanted to advertise a last-minute deal for the weekend. Normally we were prepared for their special offers weeks or months in advance, and this rushed project caught us at a time when we were short-staffed and extremely busy. My go-to writer for the account was Paula, a razor-sharp woman in her mid-thirties who was fast, funny, smart and dependable. She had a pile of awards for her radio ads. I knew that today, my dream girl was not sitting around on her hands. Before darkening her door, I asked Marina, the creative department manager, how Paula's workload looked. Marina checked her computer and took a long pause before speaking. She started rapidly tapping her pencil and making a staccato clicking sound with her tongue—always a giveaway she was stressed. She told me she wasn't sure the very busy writer should take it on—how about Dave? He was plenty talented as well, but he'd struck out twice on the account in the past. I told her I'd chat with my Plan A first, just to be sure, before moving on to Plan C.

Paula was deep in thought when I poked my head in. I knew she was immersed in a big credit card project, and this morning she might be thinking through anything from casting to wrestling with the latest curveball from the global team on that brand. I smiled brightly, in that way that says what you're about to hear will not make you happy. After I told her about the radio scripts dilemma, she too smiled incongruously. "I know you're busy, Paula. I thought I'd ask first, before going to Dave. He can do it if you can't make the time, you just have to tell me if it's possible or not."

Paula's arms crossed. Then her hands went to her face, fingers covering her nose as she took a deep breath. I could see a no coming. But then she said, "Give it to me. I can do it." I was flooded with relief. I knew she was the best fit for the brand, and I trusted her to pull it off. Before making my exit, I handed her the background, and shared some thoughts I had on a theme she might want to consider. I moved on to the next crisis on my list, and closing Paula's door was equivalent to putting her project completely out of my mind. Two days later, when it was time to review ideas, I would need to look at the brief again to be reminded of the details.

Paula and I slumped into couches in the creative lounge to review her ideas. I saw she had a stack of papers, and listened closely when she started to perform the scripts. Radio commercials are like thirty-second plays, and I would be judging for entertainment value (Would it get noticed, and remembered the next day?), as well as strategy (Did I hear the offer, or was it lost in the storytelling? Was it motivating, or just funny?). Paula had on her game face and did an admirable job of acting out multiple roles. You might not guess that advertising copywriters need acting skills, but selling scripts is far more effective when the author can bring them to life. Paula is exceptional at this, and I often told her, while nearly peeing myself from laughing, that she missed her calling as a stand-up comedian.

Today, however, even an Oscar-worthy performance couldn't hide the fact that the scripts were, well, terrible. Every one of them. They lacked Paula's usual attention to detail, comic timing, and insightful thinking. Even for a rush job, this wasn't presentable. My mind raced as my blood pressure shot up. As the leader, I had to make a quick decision, and I had few options. I decided the least awful course of action was to adapt an existing radio spot, to, in effect, add a "tag" that flagged the offer after about twenty seconds of generic sell for the brand. I would tell the senior client that with so little time, we would rather do this than create work below their high standards. I would manage through this fumble with an aura of confidence and conviction. Treating it as the right thing to do for the sake of the brand was a choice they could accept. Their disappointment in no new radio ideas wasn't going to feel as bad as running lame work. I hoped.

What had happened? In hindsight, that was easy to figure out. I wished I had acted on Paula's nonverbal cues instead of what she said. I heard what I wanted to hear and denied my other senses' input. It was easier for me to run off after her "yes" than to do the harder work of responding to body language that signaled this was probably too big of a stretch for my first-choice writer. Equally, I could have taken Marina's reluctance more seriously. And if I'd been really honest with myself, I'd have realized I was being manipulative when I asked her if she could do the job, bringing up Dave as my alternative; I knew her natural competitiveness would kick in. I showed poor leadership skills—essentially my choice set up Paula and the team for failure.

But what about Paula's choice? She said yes to please me. It was a win in the moment. The boss was happy. Paula wanted to retain the status of dependable, go-to writer. She was ambitious and she saw pulling off these miracles as part of climbing. Furthermore, she couldn't stand the idea of Dave stepping in. What if he did a great job? Would she now find herself competing with him into the future on this account, one of her favorites? What if Dave failed, for that matter? The guilt!

All these things went through her mind in a flash. She had no idea how she could fit in these scripts, with the credit card work already crushing. But she'd pulled off these emergencies before, and blind faith was the order of the day, she decided. The reality, though, is that far from helping, her "yes" could have bitten her in the ass. For the same difference, another creative director might have questioned her judgment, her time management skills, her maturity. There was room to wonder about her standards, and willingness to delegate. Had it happened early in her tenure, a boss like me could also wonder if she was as talented as her portfolio suggested. In the end, rather than being a badge of strength, Paula's "yes" made her look weak. I was deeply frustrated that she hadn't said no, now that I could see plainly she wasn't in a position to pull it off. How many times had I coached her and her co-workers to raise their hands if we asked them to do more than they reasonably could, when chances of a good result were nearly nil? The saving grace for Paula was that I reserved the harshest judgment for my own poor choices, and her track record spared her from a loss of status. Had it been a pattern, however, her career progress would have stalled.

By the time I started working, in the 1980s, I could easily observe many women working long and hard, and excelling. But over ten years into the achievements of the women's liberation movement (and decades after women started proving themselves to be highly capable in "men's jobs"), the conventional wisdom of the time was that a woman had to work twice as hard to be seen as a man's equal.

Decades later, women continue to say, "I'll do it. Leave it with me. Yes, yes, yes." They're still trying to prove themselves. Not that they're paranoid: in a 2010 survey of men and women on helium. com, 74 percent ticked "yes" on "women in leadership positions must work harder."[51]

So many reasons to do the wrong thing

There are other motivations to saying yes that go beyond a desire to assure the boss your gender doesn't mean you can't do it, and these can also take you down a very bumpy road. Maybe the "yes" comes because of that warm, fuzzy feeling you get making your boss happy with a can-do response, or because you are reluctant to burden co-workers with a request to pitch in, or because you fear losing status or being branded a whiner. Then there's the woman who will say yes because she doesn't perceive saying no to be an option: the boss seemed pretty black and white about his expectation. Doing the boss's bidding is a pretty normal response for most of us—even when he may be quite open to a much-needed reality check on a severe lack of time to do the task. The fear that can go along with even considering an honest discussion about a need for support or a plan B is usually misplaced. The legitimate fear is of the consequences for not declaring your limits and asking for help when you're set up for failure.

Knowing your limits is a strength. Paula's job wasn't to make her boss happy or to help me have an easier day. The rush project was really her boss's problem to manage, given Paula's lack of time to help. Paula's ideas on how to delegate would have been welcome and showed leadership. I would have respected her decision to draw a line.

The price you pay

When a yes should be no, it's self-sabotage. For your can-do answer, you will often face big problems later, because you're going to wear the bad results. And your poor choice impacts others. Paula's yes meant the whole team was tarred; blowing deadlines is a mega-sin in any business, and no client is happy to hear the day before a presentation that the job they expect can't be delivered.

A good way to up the odds of choosing the right response when you're reluctant to ask for help is to stop and ask yourself whether that gut feeling you have that you won't be able to deliver anywhere close to your best suggests you'll pay later. Shift your focus from the initial, grateful smile from the boss to the end result, and be honest about it. Do you have conditions for success? Will he be smiling later?

Look back at the results you've had in the past year. Did you do your best most of the time? Hardly ever? How often did disappointing results connect to you saying, "I can do it," when you knew you were in over your head? Now consider what would have been the worst that could have happened if you'd raised your hand for help or said no. If you're an employee known for a good work ethic, the penalty won't usually be much worse than fleeting frustration from your boss. It's unlikely that you'll suffer consequences for being honest while declaring commitment to doing your best.

Put another way, make sure you have what you need to succeed. Given the goal, can you deliver without help—or at all? What would you need? That's what the boss needs to hear: "I can do it if I can get an intern to assist me (or a bigger budget, or one more day)." Tell your boss what you can do within the parameters given: "I can't deliver three new options in the time frame, but I could create one."

Your boss has a plan B, C and D

When you take that deep breath and declare the truth, know that your boss is likely more prepared to deal with your dilemma than you think. He probably knows he's pushing his luck and has been for years—ever since downsizing led to one employee being asked to do the job of two (or more). I'd be tempted to suggest sympathy for the leader who's at his wit's end managing with so few staff, if it were remotely your problem as the employee. Regardless of their constraints, if you tell them you're at full capacity, unable to take on the request, they will find another plan. You can't be labeled a slacker when you explain your workload or another conflict with getting it done. When you deliver the bad news, it can be especially effective to paint a picture of the bad outcome you anticipate, to underscore the risk of going ahead. Tell the story that would keep them up at night if they were to follow through, and the need to shift gears will become obvious. They'll get you more resources, change deadlines or simply find someone else. Draw a line in the sand and be amazed by how well it works.

Most leaders aren't on top of each employee's most current reality, so you need to make it your business to be sure they are. It's a smart long-term strategy to meet with your boss with some regularity for the express purpose of updating her on your bigger picture—the good and the bad. This is part of managing your career. Most people think the boss is bound to know everything. Starting right this minute, assume they don't. They have their eyes on a million details. Note: management is also spread too thin. Make sure you're not a mystery. And when you have problems to share, always show up with ideas for how to solve them. Put simply, doing all you can to have conditions that enable your best performance will assure you advance—and mean better results for your company.

Shooting holes in "can't"

Nine years ago, I found myself in a situation where asking for help seemed out of the question, but I had never needed it more.

I had just reconnected with a former Kraft Foods client, Zo Ratansi. I had known him as an intuitive, big-picture thinker when we worked together, and now, he was in a brand-new career in corporate team development and coaching. His true calling was not marketing Kool-Aid. Zo was enlisted by his former employer to facilitate healthy dialogue between the marketing teams at Kraft and its longtime ad agency on issues we struggled with. He and his partner did a near-miraculous job of leading our two groups to the root causes of chronic logjam, and after one long day, we left feeling that we could all work together more productively. A few days later, I heard from Zo.

"Nancy, you seem very unhappy."

"Well, um, yeah, I guess . . ."

"Let's have lunch and talk about what I could do for you."

I balked. The thought of "life coaching" was a big eye roller. I had an image in my head of Tony Robbins–esque you-go-girl cheerleading. Not my thing. But a day later, after thinking about his frank—and accurate—take on my mental state, I agreed it couldn't hurt to talk.

By the end of that lunch, I'd done a 180. I had a very different mental picture of what coaching could mean for me, and was eager to begin a series of sessions. Feeling a little self-conscious, I approached my boss to broach the subject of the company covering the expense. I was now so excited about the prospect of getting this form of help that I got past my reservations. It turned out my company wasn't new to supporting employees with life coaching, and so I began an experience that I consider a turning point in my life.

My daughter, Lily, was a shy eleven-year-old about to start seventh grade in a new school. She was also about to begin a new living arrangement. For the first time since her parents had separated, she would begin splitting her time between us. For six years, she had seen both of us every couple of days.

Like many people with failed marriages, I felt tremendous guilt about the impact of divorce on my child, compounded by the big job dilemma: I was not the stay-at-home mom that Lily's friends all appeared to have. (Our Toronto neighborhood, "The Beach," is like a small town from the 1950s in many ways). I was a single mom with a supportive ex-husband who played a role more akin to Mom than I did. One day, I was driving Lily to school when she said to me in a matter-of-fact tone, "I'm never having kids. I'm going to be a vet, so I know I won't have time for looking after a child, either." I was shattered. The illusion I had that I was managing work and home life admirably instantly vaporized. My daughter was entering an unnerving, overwhelming new stage of her life, and she felt her mom wasn't there for her. She was becoming more withdrawn as the calendar neared September, and I was in a state.

Sitting in a small, out-of-the-way office on a Monday afternoon, Zo asked what I wished I could change about my life the most. I didn't have to mull that over; I said I wanted to put 100 percent of my focus on Lily at this turbulent time. But I said it in the same way one might say they'd love to walk on the moon. I couldn't begin to imagine how I might do that.

He invited me to pretend there was no barrier. "So, what do you need?"

I instantly replied, "Two months off. All Lily, all the time."

"So, what's stopping you?"

I couldn't help laughing. "My boss would never give me two

months. I'm the CCO. I don't have time. I have all that responsibility, and the workload is massive. And how could I expect Janet to cover for me?"

"Would you do that for her?"

"Of course." Pause.

"What's the worst that could happen if you ask Dennis?"

"He'd say no."

The conversation was just about that brief and clear. I would ask the next day. I was emotionally prepared for a no, and I realized I could expect Janet to declare if she felt she couldn't manage.

I found, over many years of working with Dennis Stief, that he was at his absolute best in a moment of crisis. When I walked into his corner office at the appointed hour and closed the door behind me, he undoubtedly expected some kind of bad news. His demeanor was calm and relaxed, though. He invited me to take a seat. In the distance, white sails dotted Lake Ontario, and afternoon sun brushed the water. "So what's up, Vonk?"

I told him I had a personal problem at home, related to my daughter, and not much more detail than that. And I hoped he could support a two-month leave of absence for me to work through this rough patch. He didn't press for more details or challenge me to consider how hard it might be for the company to manage through my absence.

"Leave it with me. I'll get back to you soon."

For Janet, who knew everything as a best friend would, it was clear how badly I needed the time. She didn't flinch. This would be tough to manage through, though she wouldn't admit it until years later. And by then, she was glad she had done it for the new management skills she'd picked up while flying solo—in particular, delegating.

I got near-instant approval from the company. My CEO compared notes with Janet and then head office in New York, and it was done. They wanted to support their valued employee. Dennis said he hoped I'd be back in two months, much the better for the time away.

A personal crisis stood between me and good leadership. Zo helped me see the obvious: I wouldn't be penalized for asking. Once I got past my initial fears, I saw no difference between my leave of absence and a man's medical leave or sabbatical. It was critical for my well-being, and I returned to work in a far better state of mind after Lily's dread of her big changes started to melt away. Our relationship got to a much better place. My two months off didn't spell disaster at the office. Not only did everyone live, that year Ogilvy Toronto had one of its best years to date.

Asking for help is a sign of strength

Today, Janet and I coach people to reframe "asking for help" as "asking for what you need to succeed." That's exactly what I suggested to a woman I met in Atlanta not long ago. Suzanne was highly accomplished, but a blinding smile couldn't quite hide that she was stressed out of her mind. She confided that she had suffered two huge losses just months apart in the past year: her husband of ten years had walked out and the grandmother who had raised her had passed away. Suzanne hadn't taken time off work after either loss. She explained that she didn't want to let down her equally overworked partner, and feared losing status if she showed weakness. She assumed her request for time off would be seen as a lack of mental toughness. As a woman with ambition, she thought any question marks around her coping skills would stand in her way. I feared that the superhuman effort it had taken for her to appear to take these devastating setbacks in stride was now about to catch up with her. I was grateful she confided in me, so I could assure her it was appropriate and critical for her to make her well-being the priority now. As I had learned myself, most companies will approve a reasonable request for badly needed time off or provide other support in a crisis. She was able to regain her footing not long after she asked for the help she needed.

Your own deeply ingrained reflex to tough it out alone may be hard to change, but you can kick it. When it's time to raise your hand for help, do it for yourself, and everyone else.

"Team" beats "hero"

In some cases, it's not a fear of looking weak that keeps women from asking for support from others. There are times when collaboration with a group is something you're hoping to avoid, because you want the credit for solving a problem by yourself.

The classic business model across virtually all industries features a hero, the individual who *wins*. We respect (and envy) the one called out for his exceptional accomplishment, and he goes on to get his name in lights, the raise, the promotion. In our business, *Mad Men* does a fairly decent job of portraying the stereotype. The Big Idea is produced by one person.

It's most common in ad agencies to have just one chief creative officer. Janet and I decided to share the role because, at first, we didn't think our life circumstances supported either of us taking it on solo. But more than that, we recognized the value of collaborating. We've shared the credit and doubled the reward. And we encouraged the teams we mentored to not only ask for help when they needed it, but also to look for creative ways to collaborate at every turn.

Some of the agency's greatest successes came through collaboration. A particularly challenging project we faced in 2007 leaps to mind. Our Kraft client was desperate. Their sixty-eight-year-old product Shreddies (a plain, square wheat cereal) had been in decline for ten years. After ruling the Canadian cereal roost for decades, Shreddies was running on fumes, drowned out by the chocolaty, sprinkled and popping alternatives that always seemed to have news ("Now with a fruity center!") in a category that depends on it. Shreddies had none. Kraft was close to pulling the plug on marketing support for "Good, good whole wheat Shreddies."

When we sat down with the team leader at Kraft, she was open to trying something new after our frank observation that the current processes at both Ogilvy and Kraft weren't exactly leading to brilliant results. Among them was relying on a single, senior creative duo to solve the problem. We needed radically new thinking and we wanted to open the task up to many more perspectives. We would look to the Avengers' model—if Iron Man, Captain America, the Hulk, Black Widow and Thor were able to save the world when they joined forces, a superhero advertising team could save Shreddies.

We assembled a diverse group that included the youngest (an intern), two senior art directors, a planner who was well versed on the brand and one who knew nothing about it, and two people from the digital group. From outside the agency walls, we included the most junior of the Kraft marketing team in much of the agency process and, later, a comedian. Where normally a senior pair would take the challenge and go off to generate ideas, we started a collaborative, creative process before there was a formal "brief" with our unlikely-looking group. We had fresh research from our clients that revealed our "target" still liked Shreddies, but they thought about it less than, say, the expiry date on the Arm & Hammer at the back of the fridge. So we knew our challenge was to get the brand back in their heads.

With the combo of deep experience and none, many areas of expertise and left- and right-brain thinkers, a simple strategy emerged quickly: let's make Canadians talk about Shreddies. Hmm, when was the last time you talked with a friend about a cereal? Never, of course. What would that take? We identified this big, impossible-sounding goal, and from there, our group began a new pattern: they'd form smaller groups and go to separate corners of the office to work on the problem, and then regroup over and over again to compare notes, cross-pollinate thinking and build on what emerged together. The senior people had some great ideas, like putting massive posters on tall buildings, which made no sense until you got to just the right point in your drive along Toronto's main roadway, when one singular image would come together: the Shreddies box. (An art director painstakingly created a miniature model to demonstrate the dramatic effect.) But ultimately, the summer intern cracked it wide open. When Hunter Somerville had the idea to create a fake new Shreddies flavor called Diamond Shreddies (tip the square on its side to take it from "old, boring" to "new, exciting") we recognized our winner, scribbled on a piece of paper he later said he almost didn't show us because "it was so dumb."

The next step in moving forward from his scribble was putting Hunter in the midst of seasoned creative leaders who could run with all its potential—pushing it into TV, print, outdoor and online. The team that would mine the Diamond Shreddies comedy gold kept expanding. We invited the comedian who had once taught Hunter improv to not only play a research moderator in a real focus group ("Diamond or square? Which do you think is better?") but to collaborate with the agency on how to capture the best footage of the focus groups for online videos. The sixteen interviews were done completely authentically to show the research that's typically conducted to get people's response to a new product. The unwitting participants were told afterward what we were really doing. They were such good sports that all but one was game to be included in the campaign. As the interviews continued through the day, on the other side of the glass, our intern, senior art director Ivan Pols and the young client brainstormed about more ridiculous questions. ("It's like a six and a nine: they look the same, but they're very different," the moderator said at one point. "Yes, or an *M* and a *W*," a woman offered gamely. "Right!") What began as an inexpensive day of shooting videos for the website became content for TV commercials, and probably the funniest part of a standout campaign.

A really exceptional ad campaign that started with the most junior person trumping the seniors necessarily began with bruised egos. We expected the seniors to get past it and collaborate with the guy who would more typically be bringing them coffee. After some initial balking, they got on with it, and it wasn't exactly torture. They built on a good premise and made it great. The intern got a priceless education, and there was huge payoff from the talents of the whole team being in play.

Another person who turned out to be key to great collaboration was the young member of the Kraft marketing group. By inviting him to see behind the curtain and even participate in the creative experience, we gave him new understanding of the workings of an ad agency. And he was a cheerleader for the idea with his boss, the senior, conservative woman who both loved the idea and felt certain terror. For her, putting millions behind a joke that might not land well was a huge risk. With a co-worker framing the idea and its merits in her language, she felt more conviction that this was a concept grounded solidly in good business sense. She was persuaded it could get lots of publicity for its outrageousness and get Canadians to think of Shreddies when they hit the cereal aisle.

The Diamond Shreddies campaign went on to prompt massive sales, with talk value fueled by raging debate between the surprisingly large number of people who didn't get that it was a joke and the majority who thought it was hilarious. This played out online, and Kraft fielded a pile of complaints ("Do you think we just fell off the turnip truck?") with good humor. The team was inspired by the complaints to go on to create another leg of the campaign, shot in the office of our CFO. The fictitious president of Shreddies read actual complaint letters and tried to diffuse the "public outcry" with coupons for "The Combo Pack" (half diamonds, half squares).

By this time, the collaboration of a big team was a well-oiled process for Kraft business. Our clients were open to considering almost anything we showed up with, as their sales were great and we'd earned their trust. Diamond Shreddies won a prestigious Grand Clio, and the intern landed in the pages of *Maclean's* (admittedly, on a slow news day). A three-page article documented his Cinderella story. The irony in our favorite example of collaboration is that he appeared to many to be the singular hero. But in fact, everyone involved saw their careers ramp up, with all their names attached to a great campaign. Both Ogilvy and Kraft embraced this new kind of "let's all help each other" model, and to this day, we use the case study as evidence that a diverse collaboration put against solving any kind of problem is usually your best foot forward.

Combining forces

Working collaboratively can help you achieve goals that might not be possible on your own. Dr. Barbara Cook began her medical career as a somewhat insecure, frustrated medical resident working in small-town America. She credits collaboration for her rise to president of Johns Hopkins Community Physicians.

Dr. Cook got her medical degree later than most, her destiny as a physician delayed by a discouraging father who told her point blank she wasn't bright enough to make it. After years of leading a life of service alongside her migrant minister husband that started with John F. Kennedy's new Peace Corps, she found herself in deep depression. Therapy made it clear that her subverted desire to be a doctor could no longer be denied. Pushing forty, with three young children, this woman turned her life upside down and redirected her energies toward a huge new goal.

A résumé featuring an undergraduate degree in music, a stint as a union organizer and science credits from a community college didn't impress at most medical schools. Barbara finally prevailed at the Saint Louis University School of Medicine, where she did her interview with the Hispanic dean in fluent Spanish in a bold or foolish effort to stand out. ("Mrs. Cook, you are not normal. And maybe this school needs more people who are, well, different.") Nights already spent up late with a baby now included the heavy workload of studies. She made it happen, and the "average," "old" student not only graduated but quickly proved to be an exceptional physician.

And yet this ambitious woman still found herself at a loss, right out of her residency training, working for a male administrator in a remote town in West Virginia. A new hospital had been built several months after her arrival, and spaces were designed for the typical hospital functions. There was one glaring omission: he hadn't included dedicated space for the physicians to consult with patients. When this was brought to his attention by Barbara as well as two other female physicians, each found their recommendations fell on deaf ears time and again. He moved no further than suggesting that the doctors could work in the hallway "or perhaps in a corner of the morgue." They all felt defeated and powerless. And they were infuriated as they saw that the boss readily responded to the ideas and requests he received from male physicians.

When these women finally compared notes and collaborated, things changed dramatically. On opening day for the new hospital, as Barbara tells it, the boss came to work to find the three physicians he had blown off countless times, with arms linked. They wore vintage army helmets and stood in front of what had been the hospital gift shop hours earlier. Now it was office space dedicated to serving patients, without a teddy bear or get well card in sight. The women looked straight at their speechless leader and said, "Won't you come in?" Overnight, with the help of a sympathetic maintenance crew, they'd turned it into a welcoming place for patients to meet in consultation with their doctors.

Together, these women found a new level of creativity in problem solving, and the formidable power of joining forces. As Barbara advanced at other hospitals, she took the lessons of collaboration with her. One of the most valuable lessons was that working with other smart women meant quicker, better decision making.

Finding your dream team

Dr. Cook and her female partners had complementary skills and ideas. Simply being the same gender didn't assure they would achieve their goals. The dynamic of any group with a shared mission has a big impact. Chemistry makes a difference.

You may not find yourself on the ideal team for your best efforts, or on any team, for that matter. If not, don't wait for fate to rectify the situation. Seeking out the group you really connect with will make the job more interesting, productive and fun. You're more likely to do your best and advance faster. So if you're interviewing for a new job, meet the people you'll work with the most closely before signing on. Like a blind date, it will allow you to get a sense if something special can happen, or if it's a train wreck in the making.

If you feel you're stalled in your current job, the right people around you could make the difference. Who inspires you most? Investigate ways you could work more closely with them. Nothing keeps you from informally spending time around them to compare notes on work, share ideas or ask for advice. This can be the start of collaboration that works. Ultimately, if you think you could do better in a different group, consider this: the boss wants people to deliver their best, so he is usually open to any ideas his people have that can lead to better outcomes.

At first glance, the group model of problem solving may not look as sexy as the hero model. But The Avengers beats any single hero, any day—even Iron Man, my favorite. Link arms with a good group and go for world domination.

Darling, you can't do both.

Mark Hilltout came to my office and closed the door, a sure sign something big was up. (The entire time I worked at Ogilvy, closing a door almost always meant something IMPORT-ANT was about to be said. As a card-carrying pessimist, my assumption was that the important thing would probably be bad.) My boss lit his first cigarette of the day, took a long drag and got straight to the point. His time in Canada was up, he said. His wife, Sylvie, was restless, and he was ready for a different challenge. He had accepted a job at Ogilvy's head office in New York.

This was indeed bad. I loved him as a rare, truly great boss is loved. He had grown me from dirt. Mark had hit Ogilvy Toronto like a Category 5 hurricane two years after I started working there. The British creative director had arrived from Hong Kong on a mission to raise the standard at an office that had been turning out *meh* work for several years. Mark's course correction was swift and painful. Many of my co-workers headed for the exit. But the man I often described as John Cleese's younger, better-looking brother hired Janet as my new partner and ultimately became one of our biggest champions, pushing us into more senior roles and teaching us how to create work that was miles better than anything we'd done before. Now, three years later, we had come to respect and adore him.

I felt a little wave of nausea as he described his new gig. But if Mark's headline was a shock, the next thing he said was a bigger one: he thought I should take his place. "You have everything it takes to lead. You're the whole package. You've come so far, and I'm so proud of you. This is what you were meant to do."

I didn't believe I had the ability to lead a policeman to a donut. I felt I lacked the gravitas, charisma, and fundamental ability to do the job. I practically turned around to see if there was someone behind me who fit the description. I was struggling to absorb what he was saying when he moved on to share a piece of advice, should I accept the big promotion. He leaned forward with serious brown eyes fixed on mine and told me *I really shouldn't have children*. "Darling," he said, "you can't do both."

For just a moment, I felt amused by Mark's outrageous political incorrectness, but then I became deeply annoyed. Mark himself had three daughters and a wonderful Belgian wife, who was a talented photographer and stay-at-home mom. I assumed he thought it went without saying that this was the natural order of things. Like all the other male leaders I knew, he had the option of children because, of course, Mom would be on top of the kid thing.

The big fade-out

As jaw-dropping as my mentor's 1993 advice sounds, today's data suggests an awful lot of women and their employers don't believe they can do both. In a 2010 study of University of Chicago MBA graduates, researchers found that 13 percent of women graduates had dropped out of the workforce nine years after graduation, compared to just 1 percent of men.[52] In another study of sixty Fortune 500 firms, management consultancy McKinsey found that while more than half of all entry-level employees were women, the proportion dropped to less than a fifth in the C-suite.[53] When Janet and I think back on the number of women we started our careers beside compared to the number of women who went on to step into senior roles, the list of those who jumped off the ride could fill this book.

Today's reality is that in spite of swelling numbers of women in schools and professions of all sorts, huge numbers leave the career track to have children. And they don't generally return to continue on their pre-baby trajectory, if they return at all. They may preemptively lower their expectations, fearing the obstacles to managing those two full-time jobs will be too great to pick up where they left off. Sometimes they succumb to gravity when they work in environments that make them feel they're no longer as valuable. Whatever the reasons, the exodus of women from the path to more senior ranks isn't letting up. During our thirteen-year tenure as CCOs, finding a senior female art director or writer was often like looking for leprechauns. Aside from a very few well-known teams, they didn't seem to exist.

When women do step into high-profile top jobs, the news flash isn't always entirely celebratory. You no doubt recall the headlines when Marissa Mayer became Yahoo CEO in the summer of 2012. There was applause for Yahoo's decision to bring on the wildly creative thinker behind so many Google milestones. Yahoo went for talent and was undeterred by the temporary complications impending motherhood would add to the picture. But the loudest voices suggested that being pregnant should be an automatic "need not apply" for the top job. Yahoo was criticized for making a reckless choice at a time when a "fully committed" CEO was required. The old narrative continued: if you're a woman with children, you're going to be distracted.

Then there's this kind of story, from the investment sector, to keep ambitious would-be moms wondering what to do: Carley Roney, co-founder of XO Group, a publicly traded media company worth an estimated $300 million, told *The New York Times* that while venture capitalists will claim that a woman entrepreneur's pregnancy won't influence the decision to invest, "behind closed doors it is a factor."[54] This reality is what prompted her to keep her baby a secret in the early stages of her business. Maybe it's no wonder that so many young career women worry about the career implications of having a baby.

Shortly before becoming a CCO, I was in a huddle at a Toronto bar with Kara Goodrich, one of America's most awarded copywriters. We'd just spent the day judging Canada's Marketing Awards, and I was showing Kara a picture of my young daughter. Looking at the photo, Kara suddenly got very serious. "How do you do it?" she asked. She wanted a baby but wondered if her value would drop when she became a parent. I was floored. This brilliant young woman was undaunted by creating world-class work that made millions for clients like Keds, Polaroid and United Airlines. She took her industry's onslaught of accolades in stride, year after year. Any agency in the country would have killed to hire her. But one of the most employable people in advertising was completely unnerved by the thought of what having a baby might do to her career.

Taking the plunge

Right up until my mid-thirties, I had spent virtually none of my time worrying about whether or not I could manage parenthood and a career, or the bias women can face when they start a family. I had no desire to play Mommy. I had never felt the slightest twinge of maternal instinct—even as a little girl, I was only into dolls for the hairstyling opportunities.

If my biological clock was ticking, I didn't even notice it. But I had promised my Dutch husband I'd take a leap of faith and have a child. Some day. Parenthood was a prerequisite for our marriage three years earlier. "Some day" came thanks to Mark's vexing appeal to skip children. I've always had a contrarian reaction to anything that smells like an ultimatum. Happily for me, my husband and my daughter, Lily, this got me off the fence. Just a few months later, I stood in my bathroom staring at a little vertical line on a home pregnancy test. It felt as if I was at the top of a very steep roller coaster. I didn't tell Mark of my revenge pregnancy until I was almost five months along. He could not easily feign happiness for me. I remember his tight smile.

If I couldn't do both, I didn't much care. When I left work to have my baby, I thought everything was tickety-boo. I was happy with my status as an associate creative director. I had job security, savings for the time off, and I was certain I wasn't missing a thing by taking a pass on the top job. The only thing that wasn't totally perfect was my nagging fear that I might turn out to be the worst mother ever. Shouldn't I be bursting with excitement and anticipation rather than filled with dread? Nine months pregnant, the size of a house, I still didn't feel maternal. Had I waited too long, now so set in my childless ways I couldn't adjust? Would my child be a serial killer one day, owing to a cold mother?

My fears turned out to be a tad overwrought. Two days into motherhood, I fell hard for Lily. In fact, I can remember the exact moment the maternal love kicked in. When we left St. Michael's

Hospital after a perfectly awful stay sharing a room with a new mom who screamed at her husband on the phone at all hours, it was raining. As we got into the car and I clipped Lily into the car seat, I felt a wave of protectiveness for the newborn mini-me in my arms. It was a new emotion for me, foreign but wonderful.

I took only three months off, which was a good thing financially, as I had grossly overestimated how far my savings would go. Life with a new baby, house and car: not priceless. I had no choice but to get back to bacon delivery. But if I was a blubbering mess on my first day back at work, soon I was in a way better place, with the consolation of being able to go to the bathroom and eat lunch at will. I also found pretty quickly that career plus motherhood was a satisfying combo for me.

Career, interrupted

My quick return to "normal" wasn't exactly normal. Many new moms experience numerous challenges back at the job that are usually more nuanced than dead obvious. Most workplaces reward time spent in the office, and research suggests men just have more of it. The University of Chicago study of MBA graduates that I mentioned earlier found that women with children worked 24 percent fewer weekly hours than the average man. In fact, the researchers said, "the presence of children is the main contributor to the lesser job experience, greater career discontinuity and shorter work hours for female MBAs."

They also discovered that any career interruption of more than six months takes a huge toll on not only earning power but also career advancement. Not surprisingly, women are 22 percent more likely than men to have a career interruption within ten years of graduating. After having kids, many of those female MBA graduates decided to leave the path to their original goals. Instead, they chose "family friendly" jobs that had shorter hours, reduced pay and—surprise—less opportunity for career advancement. Facebook COO and *Lean In* author Sheryl Sandberg might call this "leaning out"—taking themselves out of their careers—because they essentially bought into making a tot-or-top choice.

When Ellen Ma was climbing the corporate ladder as a director of marketing for a national retail chain, she took one look at the nonexistent work-life balance of some of her female colleagues and figured that career plus children wasn't in her cards. "I could barely manage myself—I didn't want to introduce a family into it," she says. Her only friends who were able to swing the mom-career combo either had loads of backup from relatives, or the money to pay a staff of housekeeping and child-minding helpers. At the time, Ellen had neither. So she opted for top, not the tot. She said, "I saw them struggle. Yes, maybe the outcome would be great. But I always felt the journey should be pleasant, and I didn't see any enjoyment in all of that." When she relocated to Asia, Ellen's feelings would take a surprising turn. There she discovered that the cultural norm of living close to extended family members provided working mothers with built-in babysitting—and the support to have both a high-flying career and a fulfilling family life. Had she lived there earlier in her career, she says, she might have made different decisions about family and work.

Neither of us would ever say the choice to skip parenthood is a bad one. But if you want a baby, have a baby. We've said this to quite a few young women who've shared their struggle with the big decision. If you take a pass strictly because of career fears, we fear you could have regrets. Don't let your career ambitions, negative headlines or today's pressure to be supermom stop you. Just do it. I've never met the career woman who said she wishes she had do-overs on having a child. There's always a way to work it out. Nope, it will not be a breeze. You will not be perfect. The life of the working mom gets plenty messy. But with the right conditions and creative strategies for achieving your goals, a future that includes both a decent home life and the career you want is possible. Darling, you *can* do both.

Facing down fear

Let's look at the sticky subject of Mommy Fear for a moment. No, I'm not talking about the unfounded terror we all face in paranoid moments that some unspeakable harm will befall our offspring. I'm talking about the kind of anxiety Kara Goodrich confessed to during our post–awards show huddle: the fear that motherhood renders you a lesser employee in the eyes of the boss.

Throughout the 1980s and early 1990s, Laurie Brown was a rock and roll It Girl. She was a veejay for MuchMusic. She became famous for her on-air interviews with the music elite, like Miles Davis, Robert Plant, Lou Reed. She had fun little side projects, like playing the sexy/sadistic cop in Corey Hart's music video for "Sunglasses at Night." Laurie was on a professional high when she found out she was pregnant. While she was thrilled to be having a baby, she was terrified of what it might mean for her career. She'd be the First. Ever. Pregnant. Veejay. If she could keep her job, that is.

"I thought, what's going to happen? Rock and roll was all about sex, not the consequences of it. But when I finally shared the news with my boss, here's what I heard: "This is groundbreaking. Do whatever you want." There weren't crazy camera angles to hide my expanding middle. No one freaked out. I asked for more time than I ever thought Much would give and it all worked out. I think women more often than not will be pleasantly surprised when they just open their mouths and ask for what they want. Like me, they just assume there's going to be a problem. They fear they'll be seen as aggressive, a bitch, or there will be some kind of backlash. I've found men love a woman who can say what she wants and needs." Laurie's worries didn't play out, and she has little doubt her experience can hold true for others.

Fears about how you'll manage at work—and how your kids will fare without you—are common for women re-entering the workforce after mat leave. Google's Sabrina Geremia was no different.

As the clock wound down on her eleven-month leave after the birth of her twins, she wrestled with questions like, "What's going to happen?" "How am I going to handle it with these kids?" "How am I going to develop in my career after all these changes?" But rather than putting off facing her fears until the last moment, Sabrina tackled them *while* she was on maternity leave. Three months before she was due back, she scheduled a meeting with her boss. The agenda? *His* goals. Specifically, Sabrina asked him what his top three business priorities were for the coming year. The hour-long meeting not only helped Sabrina get a handle on what had changed during her time away, it also gave her an opportunity to think proactively about how she fit into the new picture. The following month—with about four weeks left on her leave— Sabrina scheduled another meeting with her boss. This time, they discussed how Sabrina would play a role in the evolving company. As a result of that meeting, Sabrina and her boss mapped out two options. One, she could opt for her old job as head of agency relations—a "safe" role she knew and loved. Or, she could go for a newer, bigger job as sector lead, which was more demanding and ultimately, for Sabrina, more exciting.

While Sabrina acknowledges that a leap to a new role on the heels of a mat leave isn't for everyone, she encourages women to be strategic about how they re-enter after maternity leave. "Having those conversations before you step back into the building is really, really important."

The tot and the top

The professional women who, like Sabrina, go for the child, often go on to discover that motherhood can make them even better at their jobs. After my tears dried back at work post-baby, I discovered this very big, pleasant surprise: the job felt so much easier than before. Having a tot actually helped me to do well at the top.

Far from hurting me at work, motherhood actually accelerated my career. Life After Lily was not a cakewalk, to be sure. But in many ways, it was so much better. I was getting the job done; there were no complaints that I wasn't pulling it off. The quality of my work was often better, if anything. I think one reason for that was heightened empathy—a side effect of motherhood that hit even me, someone not famous for the quality. The woman who can virtually feel her child's pain can also relate more to the emotions of co-workers and clients. I was more sensitive to the feelings of others, including the target audiences for the products I was tasked with selling. If women make something like 80 percent of all purchase decisions, it seems obvious that being a mother gave me an edge in connecting with the moms.

Another new development was that I had a much greater interest in the well-being of others. For many a new parent, having a baby means not only wild interest in said baby but more concern for all babies. In my case, even great big ones that were not much younger than me: my co-workers. If I had mentored before, now I was that much more committed to helping people along. My interest in the success of others has only increased over time. I enjoy their wins as much as my own.

Becoming a mom magically shifted my orientation from me-me-me to my child and others around me. Survival of the species stuff, I suspect. I became infinitely more patient. No new parent can get through the day without patience for crankiness, crying, neediness, tantrums. Before baby, impossible to imagine coping with, but after baby, taken in stride. Okay, taken in stride-ish. At work, this newfound, deeper-than-ever well of patience was not just virtuous; it meant better coping skills.

Janet says one of the biggest benefits of parenthood for her was that it put work in perspective. If it was possible to take the job too seriously, she did. After her son, Devin, arrived, she stopped wanting to cry after every lost battle; she found her tendency to overreact and wear the hair shirt in response to failure evaporated. A little bit of distance gave her clarity. The detachment sharpened her judgment.

I wish I'd had the revelation sooner that having children can make women better at the job. And more than that, I wish this reality were accepted as common knowledge. I'm happy to see more and more press like this, which appeared in *Forbes*: "For working mothers, as for effective leaders, agility is a critical requirement. Agility means possessing strong self-awareness, emotional intelligence, flexibility, conflict management, listening and communications skills. It also means being acutely aware of how others process and respond to our own actions and behaviors."[55] And I'm also glad more and more senior women are speaking out about the value that motherhood adds to their careers.

Many women say that motherhood took their time management capabilities—a foundational skill for any leader—to a whole new level. There's nothing like having that second full-time job to bring incredible focus to the work that happens in an office. There's no choice: the working mom must learn to excel at time management. There are fewer hours in the day for work, so every hour really counts. You start to spot the stuff that can wait, can be delegated or wouldn't be worth the time.

Today, Heather Evans is Deloitte Canada's national partner for tax law, managing a team of more than two hundred lawyers across the country. But throughout the 1990s, she was an up-and-coming associate who, in addition to working full-time, also happened to be giving birth to three children and completing a master's degree in tax law. To get through the busiest time of her life, Heather had to become supremely organized. Her days were planned from the minute she woke up to when her head hit the pillow. Her daily planner was her Holy Grail, and she learned to quit relying on her memory and instead to make sure every single solitary appointment made its way there. Because time was her most precious commodity, she had to learn to make every minute count—including those career-forging hours otherwise known as "networking events."

"I didn't have a lot of slippage in my schedule. I had to be really focused on where I chose to network, who I chose to spend time with and what I was hoping to get from it." On the occasions when she didn't make it home for dinner because of an event, she always made sure she was attending something where she stood not just a good but a *great* chance of finding a new client or referral partner. Her resulting ability to transform those high-octane networking sessions into new business ultimately built business development skills that helped set her up for a top job.

Executive recruiter Cathy Preston says ruthless organizational skills are the hallmark of senior women who have successfully combined careers and kids. While many are organized to begin with, the act of balancing a lifestyle that should, by all rights, require forty hours a day helps women become über-focused.

"You have to develop amazing systems in order to run your life," Cathy says. And these systems—ranging from family agendas to ensure no important kid events get missed, to developing the discipline to go to bed at ten and get up early—become habits that help women optimize their performance at work.

One of the things we've both learned over our careers is that taking on a workplace or culture that doesn't support your life is draining work with poor odds of happy endings. It's much better to find an environment or employer that supports your success and well-being from the get-go. Our own experience suggests working at a female-friendly company beats the pants off working at a boys' club—especially when it comes time to consider parenthood.

Seeking out a company with a culture that will support your success regardless of gender makes sense on so many levels. Or, you could do like Pum Lefebure and make one yourself.

The do-it-yourself ideal environment

Pum co-founded Washington, D.C.–based Design Army with her husband, Jake, when she was twenty-nine. Her mother urged her to wait a while to have kids, but she found herself pregnant immediately after her company launched. Over the next few years, she not only raised a wonderful little girl, Sophie, but also grew a company that would go on to win countless design and marketing awards. Pum is a great example of how our beliefs shape what's possible. "I never accepted that it would be impossible to have a career and child and enjoy it all immensely," she says. "I *had* to have it all." The day Sophie was due, Pum worked until nine that night and delivered her baby at midnight. She was back at work two days later. (Marissa Mayer's two-week maternity leave was not a world record.)

Pum's superhuman ability to virtually skip mat leave isn't exactly a blueprint for the masses. But she has a very interesting answer to juggling motherhood and career: integration of work and home life. "We all have twenty-four hours. If I need to put eighty hours a week into running my company, and I want to be a good mother too, clearly, I have to do both at the same time. I don't want to do this 'balance' crap. I'd do both badly. I noticed it took my left arm to breast-feed and I had a right hand that could text. Generations X and Y are all connected. You have to be modern about it."

Sophie comes to the office after school and sits down at her own little "work station" where she can play designer, have fun with Photoshop or do homework. Jake and Pum never had day care but instead took their daughter to work events. Because many of her clients are parents too, Pum says, they always took Sophie's presence in stride. On the home front, Jake cooks and Pum cleans. They share child-rearing duties. Pum's life-work integration mantra is to put on your own oxygen mask before helping those around you. "I need to take care of myself to be a good mother. I'm very ambitious; I want to reach for the sky and I want Sophie to be right there next to me." I asked Pum if she had advice for the working mom who doesn't have the advantages of owning her own company. She shared an example from under her own roof. One of her employees told her that she expected she'd have to take a few years off to have a child, because she couldn't imagine how she'd manage both. Pum suggested her employee think about a flexible work arrangement, maybe work from home Thursdays and Fridays, for instance. "You have to be flexible with your employees," she says. "You want to keep them!" The added bonus of Pum's integrated approach to life and work: high employee-retention rates.

Entrepreneurial women might take a page from Jessica Herrin, chief executive of Stella & Dot, a jewelry company that sells its wares at home-based trunk shows, à la Mary Kay. At twenty-four, the then Stanford Graduate School of Business student launched one of the first online gift registries for brides, a company that merged with WeddingChannel.com within months. Jessica was interviewed on *The Oprah Winfrey Show*, touted as a woman who had followed her passion and found her fortune. But, as she later told *More* magazine, she had worked every night and weekend for four years straight and was growing increasingly concerned about the impact the company would have on her family life.[56] She ultimately left the company she'd co-founded and took a senior marketing job at Dell. But a few years later, the entrepreneurial bug bit her again. This time she crafted a business model that supported the family life she wanted. She told potential investors upfront to expect a slower pace of growth, because it was important to her to participate in her daughter's school activities on Friday afternoons. That didn't strike them as the end of the world, and she got her backers.

Time to get creative

When Janet and I were first offered spots at the top of the creative department, our starting point was this: "Can't do that. And don't want to." We just couldn't imagine how it would work. It was very easy to picture unhappy people in every direction—employees, clients and families all feeling they weren't getting enough of us. But we finally said yes, five years after Mark Hilltout's invitations to each of us to take over. Once the choice became working for a new boss we might clash with or taking a chance and taking charge, we turned the corner. We found our way in these roles that we were initially so reluctant to accept, thanks to a creative solution at work—sharing the CCO job—and a supportive solution at home—men who did 50 percent, often more, of the child-care duties.

Women spend a ton of energy worrying they'll be valued less after baby, and no wonder. But here's a timeless truth: great people are always in short supply. If you're valued, not only will you not be demoted, but in companies that are committed to finding and keeping the best talent, you will continue to have leverage. Janet and I were invited to speak at the launch of Women@Google— an internal program designed in part to give support to female employees, who often left when they got pregnant. In a business where change is a daily reality, they were overwhelmed, Sabrina told us, by the prospect of successfully jumping back on the ride. Google's message to their employees is clear: "We value you, and we're prepared to do what it takes to keep you."

You probably don't work at Google. Or Design Army, or MuchMusic. But we still advise you to think about what you need to succeed, and ask for it. What a concept. Approach your boss with your ideas of what could enable you to continue to deliver your best work.

Like Pum, maybe you'd find working from home part of the time, or flexible hours, would make it possible. This is becoming more common every day. (Gold medals go to Germany and

Sweden, where flextime is a feature at 90 percent of companies.) It can get complicated if co-workers feel they're picking up your slack. Good communication is key. Be transparent about your schedule to all it affects. A clear game plan understood by the team as to how the work will be getting done around your absence is vital. As well, helping out those who enable you to break away can go a long way. You can avoid making people feel as though they've been left holding the bag. When it works properly, it's the opposite of the guilt-stricken mom sneaking out to take Junior to hockey practice. Keep the reason you need to leave early to yourself—you don't need to be judged. We hope more companies copy Ernst & Young: they made flextime work for both genders by taking the parent piece out of it. Everyone has the opportunity to make flexible hours work. Karyn Twaronite, a partner at Ernst & Young in charge of inclusiveness at the consultancy, told *The New York Times*, "We moved away from fixing it as a 'woman's problem' to fixing the environment."[57]

Maybe shifting some of your accounts around or bringing in baby some of the time can work. Perhaps you have ideas for getting in-house day care off the ground. Many employers we've talked with said they're wide open to the ideas and needs of their new mothers. They don't want to lose them, pure and simple.

At Taxi advertising in Toronto, a creative director with a baby was anxious about a six-week project that would take her across the country. She asked her boss if her child could come along. Far from a hard sell, the request got a quick yes. Her boss told her "it was a no-brainer." He knew she would be happier and better poised to do her best with baby along. Win-win.

Kara Goodrich took the baby plunge; her daughter is now in her teens. Kara found a way to make life work at home and on the job thanks to the boss she followed to BBDO New York, David Lubars. He was very supportive in working out a situation that allowed her to continue to deliver fantastic work but also gave her the flexibility she needed to do the job of mom. Kara stresses that it's not all as pat as it sounds. She's a creative director, but she's set boundaries for herself and, at times, has decided to cut back on some of the duties that would necessitate more hands-on availability than she can responsibly assume. She loves her work more than ever, and some days, she feels the sting of hitting her head on her self-imposed ceiling. But the lack of personal regrets far outweighs the occasional professional ones. She has great success on her own terms.

My decision to go for the baby has been the best choice of my life. Being Lily's mother dwarfs all other life experiences. For me, it has never been a question of what's more important, the job or the child. She wins, hands down, and I missed many a meeting, trip, dinner and other work-related event when her needs were more important. Everyone lived. No doubt, my absence created some problems from time to time, but I learned to plan around it and I'm thankful for the co-workers who rolled with it. I took Lily to school every day, so I came in a little later than I did in my pre-baby days. I left by six-thirty whenever possible and worked from home later as needed. Technology is a beautiful thing.

And they all lived not totally happily ever after

Perfect world? There's no "perfect" for the working mom. The fact I was home at night by a decent hour didn't always score points with Lily, to be sure. I was there, but not really there when my focus was still on work. I was never shortlisted for the Mother of the Year award. I have regrets. Even though I tried to prevent it, there were many times when my daughter felt my job was more important than her, and that will always pain me. There were countless times when I thought I couldn't get any of it right, when I felt I wasn't doing my best for either work or child. "Balance" was a joke. But a smooth journey—balance—isn't a feature of any big career, and for me, the good far outweighs the time spent off the rails. I'm taking some comfort from Marie Curie; if this working mom could do all it took, unapologetically, to win the Nobel Prize and still pull off raising two adoring, ridiculously accomplished daughters, there's hope I won't land in Mom Hell either. (Okay, she discovered radium, I made ads. But still.)

At twenty, the young woman who often had less attention from me than she wanted while growing up has let go of some resentment. Lily's proud of her not-perfect mother and told me recently,

"You're a great mom. I have no regrets." Asked how she feels today about women taking the big job, she's all for it but thinks the other parent should be home. Well, that was her reality. I was married to a man who worked from home. He has always been more of the mom, while I was more of the dad. That's what Lily tells me. By the time she was five, we had divorced, sadly. In spite of a childhood not exactly out of a Disney movie, she's happy and we have a strong relationship. I'm forever grateful that she has a loving, committed father whom I call a friend today. He was a huge support to me through Lily's childhood. I wish I could have made the right calls every day. I wish I had no mistakes gnawing in the wee hours. But such is life. I'm glad for my choices—to become a mother and to have a satisfying job.

At the talk we gave at Google, Janet and I spoke of all the advantages mothers have when they return to work. They have so many new skills to help them make an even greater contribution; they're so well poised to step up into the top jobs. During the Q and A, one man raised his hand and asked us, "What can a man do to be as good as a mom at the job?" We were taken aback for a moment by this great question. Our answer: Watch the moms and take notes, guys. Take notes.

Stay safe.

"Will you be in NYC anytime soon? I'd love to have dinner with you." It was the creative head of a large global agency headquartered in New York on the phone, someone I knew a little and liked a lot.

"I'll be in town in a couple of weeks. Does that work?"

"Can you come sooner?" she asked. She wanted to talk to me about what sounded like a very exciting, high-level job and gave me just enough detail to make me salivate. I booked a flight.

She mentioned that there would be a third person joining us for dinner, the head of HR. Holy cow. These people didn't waste time. I made a mental list of great work stories with fantastic outcomes: happy clients, big paydays, awards. I ransacked my closet. Nothing. What would I wear to a New York dinner and interview? I'd never needed "dinterview" gear before. I flew to the Big Apple for a weekend plus a day. I arrived at the restaurant just early enough not to seem overanxious. Cut-crystal wineglasses rested on every crisp, white tablecloth. Everything was elegant, yet somehow not stuffy. Despite the presence of *very important people* at the table, the conversation was light and informal—so informal that I figured I'd been oversold and it wasn't actually anything but an early fishing expedition. The next day, as I was packing to go home, a call came. Could I stay an extra day? There were people they wanted me to meet—their president, their CEO. They trotted me out for every star in their orbit, and then came weeks of silence.

Just when I thought it had all evaporated, they wanted to discuss compensation. Their offer was three times what I was earning. But in the weeks between first meeting and offer, I'd come to the conclusion that I wasn't all that excited by the job. "But we'd be living in Neeew Yooork," said my husband, Farokh. "And that would be The. Best." He made a persuasive counterargument. I toggled between the big number and the vision of doing a job I wasn't into. The first six months would pay off our mortgage. That was motivation right there. And we'd be livin' the high life—right? Farokh was up for it.

They wanted me to be the global creative lead on a worldwide skin care brand. Could I make it like Dove? Probably not. The pressure to turn a tired old brand into a shiny newborn felt crushing. God knows what it would take to pull that off. Never mind that it was a global job. What if I blew it on a global stage? What if the hours were so long that my NYC address would be nothing more than a pillow between treadmills? What if I hated it? Or they were disappointed in me? The nasty little gremlin of self-doubt was omnipresent. What if? What if? The energy I spent deciding to turn down the big New York agency job was just as time-consuming and analytical as if I'd gone for it. But I didn't go for it. "I'm so flattered," I said, "but my husband just started a business." I made my excuses to the person who wanted to take a chance on me. "Devin is young, and friends are so important at his age. I'm happy working with Nancy. My dad is getting older."

All true. All not the reason I said no. What did I have to lose? What's the worst that could happen? Had I asked myself that good question, I might have concluded that I'd have an amazing time in New York for a couple of years, try my hardest, and if it didn't work out, I'd come home. Not so bad, when you think about it. But I didn't think about it that way. I let a boatload of fear and anxiety stand in my way. And I'd be lying if I said I haven't woken up certain nights since, kicking myself and wondering what would've happened if . . .

Steve Jobs once offered these words of wisdom to the graduating class of Stanford University: "Remembering you are going to die is the best way I know to avoid the trap of thinking you have something to lose." Most women fall into that trap quite a lot. We're the ones who whispered a dutiful no when our mothers said, "If everyone else jumped off a cliff, would you jump off a cliff?" So why don't we jump off a cliff? What are we afraid of?

Breaking a leg, getting in trouble, losing our jobs and income, blowing up our careers, messing up other people's, failing, losing credibility, damaging our kids, hurting our families, not being good enough, public humiliation, for a start. Most women have way too much of a handle on the things that could possibly go wrong most of the time. The mind-set of most women isn't the mind-set of risk takers.

What would you do if you weren't afraid?

"Women don't go into politics or out onto a trading floor as often as men. It's risky work." Kathleen Warner, former COO of Startup America Partnership, was talking about the difference in how women calculate risk. "If there's a 20 percent chance of success, they won't do it. When you couple that risk assessment with a fear of failure, it becomes tougher for women to move forward. Women have been the majority of college grads for some time now, and yet—" *boom boom boom.* She slammed her fist against her hand three times in frustration at the glacial pace of change.

Kathleen isn't alone in her view of how women calculate risk. I didn't expect to hear Kate James of Pearson say, "If I see a job description for a new role and I can do 90 percent of it, but 10 percent of it I'm not so sure about, I immediately focus on why I'm not qualified. I go into the interview and talk about the 10 percent I can't do. A guy would feel like 25 percent of the qualifications were enough and talk up those. He wouldn't worry about the other 75 percent." This is the woman who was the global head of communications for Citibank, and chief of communications at the Gates Foundation before she went to Pearson. I expected fearless, and found human.

In our work at Swim, Nancy and I have noticed that fear is the single biggest obstacle to people's progress. When Samantha's husband unexpectedly walked out on her, she was left alone with a two-year-old and a five-year-old, a New York mortgage on a house in mid-reno where they couldn't live, a rental apartment whose lease was winding down, a nanny to pay for, and a senior job with high expectations and long hours. The work yet to be done on her new home was overwhelming—floors to be laid, Swiss cheese roof to be patched, beams to be shored up—and the move-in date was getting further away. Renting by the week was a fast road to bankruptcy for her family. For months, Sam and her kids couch-surfed at one friend's place, then another's. No New York shoe box could house them for more than a couple of weeks at a time. Their nanny followed them from neighborhood to neighborhood, Sam continually mapping new routes to her daughter's school. "How do I get there from Brooklyn, from 183rd, or Astoria?" She was perpetually late for work, ducking out early, calling in sick, and short-tempered, resenting anything extra. She began to develop a reputation for being bitchy, a prima donna. It was clear something was terribly wrong, yet everyone involved took the ostrich position. Sam didn't confide, her co-workers didn't ask, her boss didn't want to know—as long as the work was getting done. She didn't expect any help or compassion from her bosses or her company, convinced they'd think less of her for the downward spiral in her personal life. Sam was sure the truth would damage her credibility more than a period of inexplicably odd behavior, so she just soldiered on. Eventually, the house was finished, and Sam and her kids became a family with a fixed address, but for months she had lived in terror of being found out and penalized rather than supported.

But wait, there's a happy ending. Once her life settled, Sam's star rose; in managing through that disastrous time, she forged in fire leadership skills that set her apart. Still, looking back, Sam wishes fear hadn't reared its nasty head at the moment when she could've used the most help.

We all have issues or problems we'd rather not share. Some are personal but have a tremendous impact on our work. Others involve clients or bosses, and we worry that taking action may put our jobs at risk. So we do and say nothing, preferring to hide in plain sight. In Sam's situation, she should have talked to someone objective—a friend, family member or trustworthy colleague or two—to try to figure out a better solution, but the fear was paralyzing, and she decided not to take the risk.

Risk reframe

I've found that jumping off a cliff requires a little mind game. I need to think in terms of leaping rather than risking. I tell myself that while risking may be frightening and dangerous, leaping is positive and exciting. Risk can look like a bad fall with twisted limbs and a broken nose. But leaping is all forward motion. It's flight. It doesn't mean you won't fall from time to time, but you'll go forward first. This shift in perspective helps me feel as though a walking cast and a few Band-Aids will get me back on my feet. It sounds childish, right? But for me, it's a tremendous way to find resolve. Learning to leap was critical to Nancy and me.

On the late-spring day in 1998 when our creative director Steve Landsberg told us he was leaving Ogilvy and suggested we "take his job, please," we did what we'd done several times before: we offered up a big I-don't-think-so. Steve's announcement was the equivalent of the floor opening up under our feet; it was saddening, unsettling. I went into Nancy's office. We closed the door and stared out at the lake. Losing Steve was tough.

"What if we . . . Nah."

"Maybe it's . . ."

"Our lives will be hell."

"Truer words . . ."

We went home that night convinced that once again, we'd take a pass. But this time, instead of vanishing into thin air, the idea started to take root. Were we ready? We weren't 100 percent, but we were less not-ready. Still, Nancy was a single parent. How could we pull it off? Did I want to do it? Could Nancy manage to do it?

"I'd consider either or both of you," Dennis Stief, our CEO said. "Of course, you'd be among several others. There are other options. We have to do our due diligence."

We made our list and checked it twice. The pros? More control; our own choices; the ability to hire; success on our own terms. And, of course, the cons: working 24/7, never leaving the job behind; having responsibility for other people's careers; facing even more pressure; having to fire; maybe missing the school play or baseball championship game; the buck stopping here—at work and at home. We'd witnessed the high-stress, family-challenged lives of our bosses. That wasn't what we wanted. How could we do the job, not lose our marbles, and still have lives that worked for us?

There was another big factor holding us back. Creative directors tend to become the face of an agency. If you succeed, you get more than your share of the credit. If you fail, you take more than your share of the blame. Either way, everybody knows. And that makes it almost impossible to step back into your old job as a writer or art director or whatever you were, if the creative director gig doesn't work out. No one wants to hire you because they worry that once you've had the control, you can't let it go. The ad community is small, and it's easier to blow up a career than you might imagine.

Ultimately, we saw it this way: the other candidates being considered were men, and we'd had as much experience as any of them.

We agreed that we'd do at least as well as the guys they were looking at, and doing it together doubled our odds of success. We threw our hats into the ring.

How did that leap pay off? For the most part, it was brilliant. We didn't always make the best choices, but in those moments of making the inevitable mistakes that are just part of taking a flyer, we reframed them. We learned to "fail up," in the words of Deena Levy, theater director and partner in various Swim programs, which means make the best of a bad situation, figure out how to turn it to your advantage, get friendly with apologizing, look for possibilities where you didn't think they existed.

Kathleen Warner had spent much of her career in law and financial services. She'd worked for a congressman in Washington. She believes strongly that women need to step up and lead. Her next step? She wanted to be where the real impact happens: the tippy top. A recruiter called Kathleen to tell her about a great organization with an opening exactly where Kathleen wanted to be. She held her breath just a little. "Do you know anyone who would be good for this job? Can you give me their names?" the recruiter asked.

Deeply disappointed, Kathleen shared a couple of names and put down the phone. "What the hell? I've got to practice what I preach. I want that job," she said into the empty room. How would she get herself on the list?

One of Kathleen's longtime advisors had the kind of influence that gets people's attention. She asked him to put her name forward.

She said, "I want to go for it. I want to lead this organization," anticipating his enthusiastic support. She was shocked when he refused.

"It's not right for you and you're not right for it. You don't have it," he said. Devastated by his harsh estimation, Kathleen did what most of us would do—she curled up in a ball for a while.

"I felt like it was because I was a woman. On paper, at least, the other people put forward weren't as qualified as me, and all of them were men. I could hardly get out of bed for days. But when I came out from under the covers, I asked myself what I'd learned. Did I approach it properly? Pitch myself the right way? What could I have done differently? What would be different if I had do-overs?"

Kathleen put herself out there and got slammed down, but she picked herself up, bruises and all, mad as hell and determined to take a lesson from it: failure isn't failure unless you give up. Kathleen took a risk that didn't work out, but if she hadn't, she might never have looked for a better future elsewhere and made her way into an even more satisfying opportunity as the COO of Startup America Partnership. Kathleen came to see that punch to her solar plexus as a favor.

Women don't just need role models for leading, they also need to see the ones who take risks, flop, and come back to fight another day. It's the way of the world. "When women do get into these high-profile situations, they feel like they can't afford to be seen to be making mistakes," Kathleen says. "Women aren't good at being public about what they've done, especially about what doesn't work out, but more of them are starting to show it and saying that it's okay to fall on your face."

There's still plenty of "but can she really do the job?" skepticism, which puts unbelievable pressure on the women who find themselves out in front. Everyone watches for failure with a beady eye. Marissa Mayer. Ginni Rometty. The number of column inches and blog posts dedicated to why they're going to self-destruct boggles the mind. Those women must feel that they have to succeed just so the army of doubters will zip it. The detractors don't stop with the über-profile poster girls for women's achievement. Name the business: if a woman is in a senior role that usually goes to a man, the naysayers are watching like vultures. So what does this tell women who want to go for it? Mostly that we'd better do it right, or else. And that's a double-edged sword. What if we wind up in "or else"? Have we frittered away our opportunity or might it matter less than we think? Maybe it's more a question of our willingness to live with the consequences and respond by getting back up.

Women do it smarter

In general, men's approach to risk is leap before you look. Like it or not, they're socialized to take bigger, bolder risks than women. The people who just "go for it" without regard for life or limb—the parachutists, snowboarders, mountain bikers, serial entrepreneurs—tend to be guys. They sleep soundly knowing that every day is an orange and they're squeezing the last bit of juice. But most of us, too keenly aware of what we could lose, aren't them—which definitely has its upside. Theater producer Brenda Surminski cast a show in which all the performers were people with spinal cord injuries. Most of the women she found had been victims of car crashes or freak accidents, like a balcony railing detaching and causing an eight-story fall. Almost all of the men had been racing motorcycles or, you guessed it, jumping from cliffs. "I had the worst time finding men who weren't injured through recklessness, and women who were."

Professor Beatrix Dart of the Rotman School translated that difference into the business context: Most men look for the great gig with the big payday, and launch themselves at it. The end. Most women feel the overwhelming need to keep more plates spinning: They want the satisfying career and the fair paycheque, but they also want time to be part of the community, to ferry kids back and forth, to attend to scraped knees, make it to a book club, and still run a household. And it affects the work they choose. In other words, women take infinitely more factors into consideration as they decide what course of action to pursue and how they're going to go about it. And this, in turn, keeps us bouncing at the end of the diving board a little longer, making us a little less quick to jump.

Donna Cohen, former owner and partner of a small, successful PR company specializing in politics, confessed that she noticed a huge difference in the way men approach risk as compared to women. "Women are much more risk averse." The words were out of her mouth without a second thought. Then she hesitated.

"Maybe that's not the right way to say it. Women are much more strategic about the risk they take."

We're more strategic, more thoughtful. Rather than feel bad about our risk aversion and fret about how it may hold us back, maybe it's better to celebrate the healthy and considered relationship women have to risk. Our less cavalier approach doesn't mean we don't take risks—just that we think them through more strategically.

The carefully considered road less traveled

Mary Anne Drummond, former head of HR for McDonald's Canada, says she has observed that women make decisions differently than men. "Men go straight from A to G if the opportunity seems good. 'It looks interesting, exciting. I'll figure it out.' But women also get to G. They just go there by way of B, C, D, E and F. It takes a little longer and they think it through a little harder. But there's a bright side to that innate caution. Women's lesser inclination toward thoughtless risk is part of what is making them so valuable to the boards they're on."

The Credit Suisse Research Institute found that in the wake of the financial collapse of 2008, organizations with more women board members were doing better. Their net income growth was greater than those with no female directors, and they paid down their debt faster. Furthermore, the net debt-to-equity ratio at companies with at least one female director was 48 percent, compared with 50 percent at all-male boards. It seems that having women on the boards did make the companies think harder about the risks they were taking and look with a sharper eye at their debt levels.[58]

I recently interviewed staff from two separate skydiving clubs who told me that women are generally better first-timers, because they want to learn everything they can about the weather, the pilot, the instructor and the instructions. They are more open, listen better and trust their crew more. Being well prepared gives them a sense that they can do it Once again, women find their own way to G.

It was bona fide, heart palpitation–inducing skydiving that gave Lisa Rodwell the belief that risk *was* for her. Rusty corkscrew curls pulled up into a bun, pink headphones on, Skype up, the newly minted CEO of Wool and the Gang sat surrounded by boxes brimming with fifty-six types of yarn, rosewood knitting needles and all the other paraphernalia needed to fill the U.K. knitwear company's chichi knit kits, as she described her relationship to the r-word.

"My sporty friend from university had the chance for a day of skydiving—was I in? I'd always made noise about doing it. And now I couldn't chicken out. Uh-oh. Up we went in groups of four, and then, one at a time, we were expected to step out and hang from the edge of the wing. I kept thinking my little weak arms wouldn't let me hang. I'm the last to leave the plane. The instructor is hollering, 'Let go of the wing.'" Lisa's heart was pounding. She couldn't stop thinking about that terrible skydiving joke: it's not the fall that kills you, it's the sudden stop. As she floated down, it felt surreal: "Blue sky above, green quilt below. They said the landing might be hard, but for me it was like stepping hard onto the bottom of a set of stairs. I just kept walking upright. Maybe it was pride that pried my fingers off the wing, but I'd declared that I would do it and I did."

Don't cling to the wing. It's advice for living that came to inform Lisa's world. Soon after the Velvet Revolution of the early 1990s, she let go of all her preconceived notions of how a girl's career ought to go. Communism gone, there was a new optimism in Europe, but the economy wasn't great and looked to be getting worse. What better time to throw yourself at a management-level marketing job in the Czech Republic, when you've never managed anything, in a country where there had never been marketing? Perfect, right? She knew she wasn't qualified, but Lisa had told everyone she knew that she'd be working internationally by the time she was thirty and her birthday was casting a long shadow. Her would-be boss, a savvy salesman-type, sweet-talked her. "You'd be bringing some-thing new not just to a company, to an entire market," he said. "It'll leapfrog your career." Lisa put her advisors on speed dial. She was on a seesaw of sleeplessness: excitement, anxiety, excitement, anxi-ety. She didn't know the market. She'd never done the job. She read about Prague. The city was so beautiful. She hurled herself into the abyss—and became addicted to leaping.

Lisa spent two years in Prague, one in London, two more in Toronto, ten more in the United Kingdom. She worked for mon-ster companies like eBay and Yahoo UK. Then Lisa went to a tiny British start-up called Moo. Her CMO at Yahoo was incredulous.

"You're leaving a great job to go to a place where they make tiny, little business cards?" Two and a half years later, she jumped to the world's best-known knitting start-up, as her taste for trying and flying continued to grow. What did Lisa instinctively recognize that a lot of us don't? That if we fall down, we'll get back up.

"I never think of it as taking a risk but rather as leaping. There's energy in taking a leap. Even if you fall, you're re-energized, and if you have to take a couple of leaps, well, a body in motion stays in motion," she said.

Kathleen Warner describes the worst mistakes of her career as having been the result of inertia. "Sometimes I stayed in a place too long. Or didn't try something because I was afraid to fail. When I acted (or didn't) out of fear of failure, that was always a mistake."

The beauty of mistakes

How often have you held yourself back because you thought you might blow it? I'd need multiple sets of hands to count the times I've done it. My mother always said, "If you're going to make a mistake, make a big one." She had a dozen different jobs when I was growing up, including flight attendant; secretary; data-entry clerk. She'd owned a French nursery school; a bed and bath store; a wool shop where, years before it was the "in" thing, she taught people to knit; and "The Pink Ladies," a DJ company named after the cocktail, where women wore pink tuxedos and the men pink shirts under their black tuxes. Our house was always an opera—

high drama as businesses succeeded and failed. Despite her example, I hate to make mistakes. *What did I do wrong? What should I have done differently?* Nothing rolls off my back. I envy men, and my mom, who are more likely to chalk it up to experience and move on. Mistakes are the currency of learning, and while they might feel like sitting on a cactus—damned uncomfortable—if you're not making them, you're missing out.

Take this advice from Sally Hogshead, who in a mere fifteen years went from novice copywriter to one of the world's foremost motivational speakers: "If you're not making mistakes, you're not putting yourself out there . . . you are not taking the sort of risks that are inherent in any degree of meaningful success. Mistakes are tuition."

Living outside the lines

To most of us, intentionally putting ourselves in a situation where we risk failure seems like craziness, yet as Malcolm Gladwell points out in his book *David and Goliath*, many successful people grew up with repeated failures as their experience from childhood on, which made them fearless. Failure itself was an inoculation against fear.

The fear of risking failure is almost as powerful a deterrent as failure itself, as Nancy and I saw in spades when we stood in front of forty of America's leading young architects, weak March sun filtering through the windows of Chicago's University Club. They'd been brought together through the Design Futures Council to develop strategies for leading their industry into the next decade. We were among the few outsiders invited to help them bust open their status quo. We'd all listened like kids around a campfire, as *Fast Company*'s brilliant, storytelling co-founder, Alan Webber, shared the tale of the city of the future that appears in the movie *Minority Report*. He said, "various high-profile architects were asked to create a vision for the film's fictitious city of the future. But they couldn't do it. Too caught up in engineering rules and building codes." Laughter rippled through the audience. They knew themselves. "The city wound up being created by gamers and architecture students."

We broke the forty architects into groups of five, promising them a surprising new way to get in touch with their endless well of creativity. We asked them to put aside all their rules, "can'ts" and fears of looking stupid for the sake of some uninhibited dreaming and old-fashioned fun. We watched the unconscious shaking of some heads. "For the next little while, let's forget that you guys are architects. We just want you to be creative problem solvers. Uncensored." In the post-lunch sugar drop, it was clear that they were dying to be doing something other than listening. We used an exercise from the great creativity coach Tom Monahan. There was a "warm-up" problem to solve: "How do you make a sandwich without bread?" They had only two minutes to come up with as many ideas as humanly possible, shouting them out, scribbling each idea on a yellow sticky note, and making the longest chain they could.

We called time. They started to share their best ideas, no matter how silly, when one talented young man raised his hand, clearly agitated. "Let's stop this right now," he said. "I don't ever want my architects showing me anything that can't be executed."

He was stymied by blue-sky thinking; he thought it was wasteful, counterproductive, even dangerous. Like the architects in the *Minority Report* story, he feared risk even in a completely imaginary context. We reminded him that this was fantasy—a demonstration that the well would never go dry and that the ideas would keep coming and coming, and that dumb ones could flip over into not-dumb ones. Nothing was carved in stone. He relaxed.

The architect found it impossibly difficult to color outside the lines. In his business, getting things right is critical. No one wants a building to fall down. Yet the city, the house, the car, the business of the future can't exist if no one is willing to pretend for a moment that there are no rules.

We have taken personal risks throughout our careers, from leaving a job with nowhere to go to telling it like we saw it to clients even though we knew we'd never win the Miss Popularity contest, from taking the creative head job in the first place to walking away when we wanted a new challenge. In the end, those choices served our careers and our clients, and even our families, even if it felt like walking over hot coals for a while. Ouch ouch ouch ouch.

So what can you do to up the odds that a net will appear when you leap?

FIRST COMES TRUST.

Trust, sometimes faith, is the thing that sets the table for risk. Working to build it is the single biggest investment we can make in any business relationship. Women are particularly good at developing relationships, but with some clients it isn't easy, so we let them languish. We don't use our natural advantage, because we're saying, "Yuck, networking" or "I don't have time." Then a moment of crisis or need arises, and suddenly it's "I need to put forward a risky idea tomorrow. I'd better have lunch with my client today." Not the ideal strategy for getting what you want.

Investing in trust was our hedge against risk. Without it, something that could have gone horribly wrong went astoundingly right. We proposed that our Dove clients create a play for a product line called Pro-Age—a real one, not a long, self-congratulatory ad performed on a stage. It would be co-created by and star thirteen women over age fifty who had never been on the stage before. We knew we were asking them to take a massive risk—nothing like it had ever been done. We held our breath as they looked at each other, communicated wordlessly, shook their heads, then said, "I love this idea." They loved this idea! There was no research to say yea or nay, no safety net. But we'd had many successful firsts together—and a few unsuccessful ones. Our long history of sharing failure, not just success, made it possible for all of us to take big—I mean BIG—chances, like throwing out forty years of "how Dove was done," creating an interactive film that was also a game (old news now, but brand new then), attacking the competition head on, letting the Dove Self-Esteem Fund mission take center stage and a big chunk of their marketing budget for a year. Our Dove clients were committed to forging a path rather than following one, and we'd delivered for them many times, using unorthodox means. But the relationship was key to that happening. Trust neutralized fear and made room for the possibility of failure without punishment. It created faith. If we hadn't had the trust, we'd never have been able to make the leaps.

In work as in life, the strength of people's personal commitment to each other is what allows you to get through the bad experiences, learn from them and move on, even though it's never fun when it's happening. Without the relationship, there's little hope of making change, or finding forgiveness.

RISK TOLERANCE STARTS AT THE HEAD.

It's true that in sticking your neck out and failing, you may find someone saying, "Off with her head." Not all bosses are good; not all environments are open to experimentation. A great boss will hear you out on what you did, so you need to know why you did it. What's the case you'll make if it goes down in flames? Taking a risk can be, well, risky, but if the reasons for doing it were sound, you'll usually get the backing you need.

Strong leaders aren't afraid of their people challenging the status quo. Many of the companies we work with today bring us in to shake things up, yet even when their leaders invite new ideas, we find fear of failure holding people back.

I won't pretend that the worst never happens, but it's rare. If you do wind up canned because it all went wrong, or because you work for a leader who expects adherence to the rules at all costs, you're probably in the wrong place anyway. Think of it as a blessing in disguise, the way Kathleen did. We've almost never seen someone sacked from a conservative company whose next opportunity wasn't a better one.

Part of the benefit of being up for personal risk is that people will go into the fight with you. It gives them the faith that they're getting your best, and that you're looking in every direction for great solutions. If you always take the safe path, they're less likely to support you when you suddenly decide to take a risk.

MAKE LIKE A BOY SCOUT.

Get as comfortable as you can with being uncomfortable, which in our case and that of many women simply means being prepared. Learn everything you can before you go for it, but don't let the fact that you can't know everything be a stopper. Channel your inner guy just a little.

WHAT'S THE WORST THAT CAN HAPPEN?

Can you live with it? Think through the risks of doing versus not doing something. It's easier to take a risk if you understand the worst that can happen. If you can live with the worst, you can leap. If you're trying to do something ambitious, you won't always be successful. But that's okay. Stumbling, falling, failing and picking yourself back up are all part of the process. Just be sure to make time for what universities call "reflections on learning." What happened? What could have gone differently? Would you make the same choice again? Then put the lesson to use. It isn't worth the effort if you don't learn from it.

EMBRACE WHAT GAVE US POST-ITS AND PENICILLIN.

Mistakes are okay. Failure is education. Just as bad ideas can be transformed into good ones, mistakes are how we figure things out. The pressure on women to look good all the time cements our fear of blowing it, and that holds us back from trying things we're not comfortable with. Worry less about the mistake and more about how you respond. We all learn to walk through tripping.

LEARN TO LOVE SKYDIVING.

Get into the habit of trying something new; it's all the better if you're not good at it. For instance, I'm not the skydiving type—I really hate heights—but just once, for a brief hour in Costa Rica, I tried to be the zip-lining type. I struggled through all my questions in fractured Spanish. "*No comprendo. Repite por favor.*" I stepped into the harness, grabbed the zip-line and got stuck two-thirds of the way across. Hanging unhappily high above the spectacular landscape, I heard them yelling, "*Tire, tire.*" Pull, pull. I got no points for style, but I made it across.

I try to understand beforehand the risks I'm taking, even if it means resorting to a foreign language dictionary. What is the potential cost? Does it outweigh the upside? Is it worth it to me regardless? How much money can I live on? What are the odds I'll actually be sacked if I take this action? How likely is it to cost the agency the account? Will it cost me my house or my marriage? Will it cost other people their jobs? Can I live with the consequences? If the answer to the last question is yes, it's usually worth it.

KNOW WHERE YOUR "NO" IS COMING FROM.

Try not to let fear be the reason you put the brakes on. If you're saying no to an opportunity because it doesn't feel right for you, you don't like the company that's making the offer, or it's in conflict with what you believe, by all means walk away. But if you "just don't feel ready," examine that with a magnifying glass. It might just be nasty, old "I can't" whispering in your ear, as it did to me when I didn't take the job in New York. If I could turn back the clock, I'd sit down with a pen and paper, honestly weigh the pros and cons, and then take a really hard look at the worst that could happen. Because it might not be all that bad. We didn't feel ready the first few times we turned down creative director jobs and we weren't. We still didn't feel ready when we accepted the job, but we were. I didn't feel ready to have a kid when I had one, but I can't imagine life without him. It all felt like risk, but it was 100 percent leap.

When Nancy and I walked away from thirteen years as the chief creative officers of Ogilvy Toronto to start Swim, we left behind some of the comforts and spotlight that came along with having a high-profile job with a lot of perks. On the one hand, there was the sense of a great deal to lose, but if you have moral support, an exciting idea and the time to bring it to life, how risky is it really?

There was a headline-grabbing story about a young lifeguard in Florida who saved the life of a man who was drowning. Excellent, right? He did a heroic thing. He should have been carried around the beach on the shoulders of everyone who didn't swim out and haul the man to safety. Instead, he was fired. He'd gone beyond the roped-off area where his company's insurance said he was allowed to save people. Crazy but true. Cue the happy ending: the lifeguard had an ocean of offers afterward.

Leaping isn't easy, but it saves the drowning man. So what if you get a little bit wet?

RULE TO BE BROKEN:

Networking is for men.

I f you want to get anywhere near the top, networking can put you in the express lane. The benefits can't be overstated. But as young professionals, we thought, like many women, that it had as much appeal as a cataract operation.

Had I been told at the outset of my career that I would need to network to get to high places, I would have said, "Well, I guess high places are not for me. Because I'm not doing that." "That" appeared to be a manly ritual where all the deals were made. The cliché I pictured: playing golf, knocking back Scotch at the club, schmoozing with people I didn't really like. The manipulation baked into networking, the aura of falseness, was a big turnoff. I couldn't justify the time (especially once I was a mother), nor did

I see myself being welcome in those testosterone-heavy settings. I believed networking was a man's game, and I wasn't missing anything; I had way better things to do. I kept my head down and assumed my work would speak for itself. My perspective wasn't exactly unique. Women in every business have allergic reactions to networking and don't think of it as important.

A few years ago, while attending a TED conference, Lesa Mitchell of the Ewing Marion Kauffman Foundation was shocked to discover that of the hundreds of entrepreneurs in attendance, only five were women. As she saw it, it was a big miss on a prime opportunity for female entrepreneurs to build their networks and form relationships with potential investors. After the conference, she began polling women entrepreneurs she knew to find out why they didn't want to attend the event. Basically, they told her, "I have a family and I'm running a company. There is absolutely no way I would spend five days of my life at TED."

Lesa has seen this phenomenon throughout her career. According to her research and experience, it's one of the reasons women entrepreneurs aren't able to raise as much venture capital as male entrepreneurs, and why women don't rise as far up the corporate ladder.

I owe a whack of my career success to the serendipity of attending a primo networking opportunity that would change my negative perceptions—eventually. At the time, I didn't see it for what it was. No one would have confused a darkened room in the belly of a Richmond, Virginia, advertising school with a golf course. But that airless classroom setting, the place where I first spent time on an ad show jury, was as surely a hotbed of networking as the eighteenth hole.

The Richmond Ad Club assembles an elite national jury to review hundreds of the best efforts of the area's ad agencies each year. The winners take home trophies that look like cannonballs, awarded for the kind of ideas that leap out from the sea of crappy ads you see every day—the very few you'd show someone because they're so clever, funny, moving or smart.

Several years into my career as an advertising art director I had never really crossed paths with any of the most influential, powerful people in my industry—the sort that are included in Richmond's judging process. And I still wouldn't have if a timing conflict hadn't forced my boss Steve Landsberg to decline an invitation to join the jury. He asked Janet if she'd take his place. It was only after neither of them could do it that Miss Third Choice got on a propeller plane to Virginia's capital.

There I was, all wide-eyed and not-elite, shoulder to shoulder with some greats I'd looked up to for years. In spite of my instinct to keep quiet to avoid gaffes, my true nature won out. Before the mid-morning coffee break, I was being my not-quiet, outspoken self. I didn't shrink from debating Jamie Barrett, a creative director famous for his work on Nike. Like magic, he and all the others became mere mortals to me as the hours passed. I felt comfortable sharing my opinions and believed my perspective was as valid as the next person's.

I didn't know I left that scene a networker. But after that weekend, I had some new behaviors. I started sending emails to people I admired, like my fellow jurors, to compliment a great piece of work. I worked on connecting people who could help each other, and I wasn't above sharing a great article or thoughts on a business opportunity with a friendly competitor. All this was networking, although that's not what I would have called it. I started reaping many benefits in return, from confidences on potential hires to insights that helped in new business pitches and even to discreet watch-outs for trouble coming on an account.

Another reward was that I started receiving more invites to join the juries of awards shows. I would eventually find out that some influential people in that room in Richmond had started recommending me to other shows; they thought I had good judgment and a good disposition for a jury. I was seen as someone with a level head in a crowd charged with emotions, and I wasn't held back by a goal to win Most Popular Juror. And, oh yeah, they noticed I was one of those very rare people in the business whom every show wants for their jury: a woman. If I thought the invitation from the Clio Awards was just great luck, I found out later I was wrong. I joined about twenty people from around the world in a less small, less sticky-with-spilled-Coke room to pass judgment on work entered by dozens of countries.

A gold Clio would send the egos and currency of the winners through the roof. I didn't leave with the coveted statue but arguably something better: more connections that I enjoyed, and the benefits of networking that naturally came along with them—like sharing insights on agency politics with a New Zealander from my company's network, lessons from failures and success, and yes, more opportunities to judge shows thanks to good word of mouth. Each show led to another.

Those jury experiences—fun outings that could reasonably have been mistaken for boondoggles—had a huge impact on my career. Now I see it: the Richmond show was the start of networking for me, complete with the snowball effect of meeting more and more influential people and all that came along with that. Nope, networking wasn't the tedious time-waster I'd pegged it to be.

Better things to do

A few years ago, Lesa Mitchell was invited to attend a premier networking event for people in the technology industry. When she arrived, she found herself in a sea of men—shades of the TED conference. Some asked her why so few women had decided to come out, saying, "We've invited lots of women, and many turned us down." Lesa gave a speech about women in technology at a similar conference some time later. She found the same situation there; the men were "so frustrated about the lack of ability to get women to show up."

According to Lesa, the very first problem is that women don't understand the importance of networks. Just like the younger version of me, many women still believe that their work itself is enough to build a great career. What's more, Lesa says that many women with networks don't understand how to leverage them.

U.K. leadership trainer Lynette Allen notes what she calls a classic example of women's tendency to undervalue the benefit of networking and get priorities wrong: in a company where a networking event was offered one evening, 100 percent of the men who said they would come made it, but 80 percent of the women who had said to count them in didn't, the most common reason given being "I got stuck at my desk." Lynette says that the responsible, reliable, big work-ethic thing is a female hallmark—and it keeps us on the sidelines. We tend to be stuck in the "right now."[59]

Some of the women we interviewed for this book suggested that—for reasons having to do with being time-starved, super-efficient or both—they feel networking is useless because it often doesn't have an immediate payoff. But we've found that in the long term, the rewards are huge. And it doesn't require a beer or a club in your hand. Networking really can be a woman's game. In some cases, it can even be a woman's survival strategy.

Venting with benefits

Lorena Knapp was on noon-hour duty in the playground at the elementary school where she taught, when a helicopter swooped across the skyline. *I want to be there, not here,* she thought. She'd had dreams of a career in the clouds since childhood, and this was the moment that tipped her into action. On her summer breaks, she started taking flying lessons. A few years later, she became a fully licensed pilot and launched her career in one of the most male-dominated industries on earth. The contrast from her teaching job—where almost all her colleagues were women—was stark. Cue the disco music: it really was raining men. Men lined the lunchroom tables, men ran the morning staff meetings. It took a while, but eventually Lorena got used to the teasing nature of most conversations, the louder volume, the palpable testosterone. But it could be tiring—really tiring. There were times when passengers balked at flying with her because she was a woman. There were other times when onlookers, having just watched her emerge from the cockpit, would ask where the pilot was. There were days she'd come home after a difficult shift, eat a quick meal and go straight to bed. "I picked my battles," she says. "But over time it just ground me down."

After a few years, Lorena realized that if she was going to make her dream job an actual career, she'd need support. So she began making an extra effort to build relationships with female pilots at her firm and others. She kept in touch regularly to compare notes, share tips, and do background research on employers. Sometimes she just vented and listened to others vent back. This network became very important to Lorena not only as a source of leads on new opportunities, but also as a support system to offer comic relief, emotional sustenance and help in dealing with the gender bias of an industry whose entire labor force includes no more than 3 percent women, Lorena estimates.

Keep it real

As Lorena's example shows, the best way to network is to do it authentically, organically, to show up without an "agenda," to meet new people for the genuine pleasure of the human connection. For us, so many good things flowed from the people we met and the relationships that formed—including finding a publisher for our first book. In a perfect storm of networking, we got a direct line to a major publisher and bookstore shelves without the usual colossal hurdles most would-be authors face.

For three years we'd been writing "Ask Jancy," an online advice column at ihaveanidea.org, a website founded and run by Ignacio Oreamuno, who you met in an earlier chapter. There were lots of common themes among the hundreds of questions we got after putting out the offer to take questions from people eager to succeed in the industry, and one day it struck us that we could shape a book around them. We bounced the idea off of Ignacio, who was also our junior art director at the time. He was quick to say, "Let's make it happen," because he felt there was a huge need for this kind of resource. But none of us had a clue where to begin. We basically sat down and asked ourselves who we knew that had some relevant expertise, who could help us, and how we could help them in return.

As it happened, this was not long after I had judged the Clios, and Amy Brophy, who now ran the show, had just asked me how I might help build the profile of the Clios in Canada. I knew Ignacio's website could advance her agenda. I made the introduction, and Ignacio agreed to create a plan to bring attention to her show. He had a fantastic surprise one day when he called her and got her voice-mail: "You've reached Amy Brophy, president of the Clio Awards, publisher of *Adweek* magazine and Adweek Books." None of us had known about her publishing connection. He sprinted into my office and said, "You won't believe it!" Because Ignacio was helping Amy with a big Toronto event, he was able to ask her about working with Adweek Books, a prestigious line of educational books for our industry. She was happy to point us to a senior editor, Richard Narramore, and her introduction meant we pole-vaulted over the gauntlet that getting to him might normally present. Then another connection came into play. Rick Boyko is our longtime friend and mentor, and our former boss when he was the North American chief creative officer of Ogilvy. A superstar in the ad industry for years and now head of one of the best ad schools in the world, he was happy to tell Richard that ours was a badly needed book that would find a large audience. Furthermore, he was in a unique position to put the school, VCU Adcenter, behind it, and pledged that he would help deliver our wish list of thirteen more heavyweights to contribute content that would bless *Pick Me* with must-read status. The deal was quickly sealed. (I couldn't bring myself to tell writer friends who struggled for years to get books published about the relative ease with which we had achieved our goal). *Pick Me* is an "evergreen" book that's become an ad school staple. If you care to, you can read it in Turkish (*Beni Seç!*). To this day, many young people approach us with their dog-eared copy in hand to thank us for advice that made a difference to them. They don't realize they're kicking off their own networking experiences in those moments. Flattered and delighted, always, we've pointed many to connections they should make.

So here's the thing: effective networking looks very little like the cliché that women find so off-putting. Keeping in touch with an Amy Brophy, a Rick Boyko, was not only enjoyable, but beneficial for everyone. They found in Janet and me people who would speak at their events, spread the word on their projects, and otherwise lend our abilities when asked. Ignacio has become a force in the industry, and he's helped Janet and me by finding talent, doing research, making introductions—the list goes on. We, in turn, invested in his company, beta tested his Giant Hydra mass collaboration concept, spoke at his events, and played sounding board for his bottomless pit of ideas. This is the perfect networking dance, support flowing in both directions. You have plenty to offer to anyone who helps you; don't underestimate the value of your own wisdom, ideas and connections to those you'd like to connect with.

Is it really networking if it all seems to unfold naturally, without effort? When it's fun, and all concerned look more like friends than "connections"? The best kind of networking doesn't feel like a chore. But unlike my unconscious approach to it, here's a thought: you should do it on purpose. And although I wouldn't say there are hard and fast rules, there are better and less successful ways to do it.

Here are some observations on making it work.

SPEND A FEW MINUTES ON NETWORKING EVERY DAY.

Many women feel they simply don't have time to do it. But if lack of time is holding you back, you incorrectly assume that you need to find hours for full golf games and nights out. If you can make a habit of carving out even fifteen minutes a day—that might mean one call or an email—you can make and maintain relationships that work. Put it in your book and think of it as mandatory.

Sean Moffitt, a word-of-mouth expert and author of *Wikibrands*, is one of the most connected people we know, with upwards of 35,000 friends across his social networks. He clearly puts a lot more than fifteen minutes into the average day to foster his relationships. But he notes he doesn't blow his brains out managing all those connections equally: he puts real focus on about 150, and that attention is woven into a lifestyle that he finds very enjoyable. He told me, "Your network impacts your happiness, health and how much affinity people have for you. You have to consciously work on it." You need not aspire to be nearly as connected as Sean, whose business model is predicated on having a very large network, but the precious connections that mean the most to you have to be maintained, like any other friendship.

Friendship? Really? Well, yeah. The professional connections that translate to introductions, greater visibility and other benefits only work when you approach them in a giving way, with genuine interest. As Sean puts it, if you fake it you're done.

THE SCHMOOZE IS AS OUTDATED AS DON DRAPER'S COUPE DE VILLE. You wouldn't begin any relationship with "I want to know you so you can help me," but that's an old stereotype of networking. Successful people know that giving something is better than receiving; it's true at Christmas and true in networking. The "something" can be anything from connecting people with mutual interests to sharing an article you know would be helpful. And it's important to do it with no strings attached. You may not get a thing in return. Mick Ebeling, who heads an international production company based in Los Angeles, is one of the most generous people you could ever meet. Without a second thought, he'll offer people he feels good about help with anything from a charity project to hammering out a business plan. He believes it all comes back to him. This six-foot-six former salesman said, "Networking becomes an extension of just loving people and trying to help them. It should be an act of giving and gratitude, come from a place of abundance, and always, always be authentic." Mick's approach ("I don't call it networking;

I think of it as wanting to get to know somebody") has enabled him to do everything from winning new business to launching the Not Impossible Foundation, a not-for-profit that began with an invention for a paralyzed graffiti artist with ALS to paint again using just his eye movement. The EyeWriter was named one of *Time* magazine's top fifty inventions of 2010. As Mick would say, don't be surprised when a generous act from long ago lands you right in front of an opportunity later.

You can ask directly for some kind of help when a relationship is established. (Mick's rule of thumb is "Give, give, give, ask.") Women aren't as quick as men to do so. Hazel Walker, co-author of *Business Networking and Sex (Not What You Think)*, and an executive at BNI, a business networking association, finds women are often uncomfortable being direct with a request for themselves, though more than happy to get it for someone else. Janet admits she'd much prefer to ask for a favor for her son than for herself. Laurie Brown waited years before she got past her deep discomfort asking for a favor. Only recently, while leading an art project for the climate change organization Cape Farewell, has she taken full advantage of her wide network. "Because I had to, there was no other way to get it all done." She had so much passion for the project that called for the help of an ad agency, film director, editor, designers, printers, an outdoor media company, PR expert, writers, social media experts and others, that she got past that sick feeling that had almost always stopped her before. Bracing herself for a series of regrets, she was instead surrounded by helping hands. "It was shockingly easy."

BE WHERE YOU'RE LIKELY TO INTERACT WITH POWERFUL PEOPLE. I had the dumb luck of being on that jury in Richmond. But you can consciously put yourself in situations where you can meet the elite. Keith Ferrazzi, the CEO of YaYa Media, kicked his networking game into high gear once he started hosting regular dinner parties for his peers—always with the request that one of them bring along a guest "a couple of levels up." In time, his dinners became renowned for their great guests (always seated in ways that led naturally to common ground and new friendships), and today the entire guest list is "a couple of levels up" and always a coveted invitation.

You may not land at Keith's table or travel, like him, in a first-class seat on your next flight ("I always travel first-class—that's where the decision makers are"), but there are other ways to put yourself where people with power and influence are naturally likely to be. Our friend Daryl Aitken, who has held leadership roles at eBay, ad agencies and fashion retailer Eaton's, says she does things like saying yes to joining the board of WWF and chairing industry events. These activities align with her interests, but they also give her the opportunity to meet accomplished leaders. She says that one of the best choices she made was attending The Judy Project several years ago. Among the many benefits of the program was leaving with connections to exceptional people that help her to this day, notably in the form of a personal advisory board she can tap into whenever she can use good feedback and advice.

Volunteer your help for causes you are passionate about. On top of the feel-good reward, the generous, powerful people who run and chair these organizations can meet you in an ideal context: you'll be showing what you're made of while helping the cause, and them. They'll be happy to help you in return.

You can also use second-hand networking to connect with the big and massively influential. Turn shamelessly to your friends who have connections that can help you. My friend Diana called me to ask if I could give her a crash course on Toronto's former mayor David Miller—he's the chairman of the board of a charity I work with, and she had an upcoming interview with him to pick his brain as she searched for a job in his area of interest. She was able to show up to the interview, feeling confident and comfortable, and in turn, he was generous and helpful. To do our homework for this book, Janet and I turned often to Amy Cross, who has a massive network of women in high places through Vitamin W, a news site for businesswomen. We met Amy in the first place thanks to asking our super-connected publisher friend Sarah Scott to help us cast a wide net.

BOLDLY GO.

Marva Smith Battle-Bey, president and chief executive of the Vermont Slauson Economic Development Corporation, told *Diversity Woman* magazine that, in her opinion, men are more comfortable networking, and establishing who they are by point-ing at what they've done. "They more easily discuss their accom-plishments. Many women are uncomfortable talking about what they have done and can do." Hazel Walker says this is a real lim-itation when you're hoping to impress. "Men speak to impress one another, and women speak to relate to one another," she told *The Globe and Mail.* That can lead to a weak exchange when women network with men.

When there's an opportunity to approach an exceptionally accomplished person, women are exceptionally tongue-tied. I lived the nightmare. My very first meeting with Mayor Miller was a disaster. At a networking event for people about to attend a week-end workshop for Cape Farewell, I was speaking to a woman who looked like a friendly stranger in a crowd I didn't know. Over the din, I learned she was a lawyer. Several moments into our small talk, David joined our little huddle and slipped his arm around her. Ah, Jill was his wife. I was so flustered to suddenly be standing next to a personal hero that I felt that I had to contribute something, I don't know, *worthwhile* to the conversation. I lurched into the incredibly not-interesting topic of listening skills, which I'd just taught at a leadership workshop. To my horror, even as I spoke, I realized I sounded as if I was coaching Mayor Miller on how to be a better listener. It was like one of those nightmares where you're naked in front of the class, and you can't wake up. I didn't know how to pull out of the topic. There was massive relief, I'm sure, when I finally, abruptly and awkwardly, backed away from the table. "Okay then, I'll be going now." What's the worst that can happen when you try for smart, light banter with a big person? Something like that. And I'm proof you can later redeem yourself with that same person, if it really matters. Like he cared.

Steve Mykolyn, a partner at Taxi advertising, puts men's relative ease in meeting the elite down to the prom. "The universal truth in our culture is that the teen boy has to face down pure terror to ask the girl to the big event—that cute girl who could shoot him down in flames within seconds. There's no getting around that milestone. Once you've lived through that, no approach to someone intimidating is ever as scary again." Well, *there's* a different theory! Steve has connected with people from his industry's legends to rock star Robert Plant to Bill Clinton, with no knocking knees or peed pants. His low-key approach to celebrities with shared interests has brought their crucial support to his charities and art projects. From his first attempt as a journalism student to get an interview at the inaugural Toronto International Film Festival ("Hello, Mr. O'Toole! I wond—" "Fuck off."), he learned that "f*** off" comes with the meet-big-people territory, and for him, it really is no big deal. Steve turned around and asked the less belligerent Donald Sutherland for some words and got his article. ("Janice says no to the prom, but Ann, one locker over, says yes.") Steve said, "Women ask themselves, 'Why would he want to talk to *me*? And it will be so embarrassing if he blows me off.' As kids, women never had to face the fire like the boys did. They were expected to be demure and not put themselves out there. The man who walks right up to Bill Gates to say hello really doesn't much care if he gets the cold shoulder, let alone from people way down the food chain from that." Steve's prom theory may not be exactly scientifically validated, but his basic points ring true. As Wayne Gretzky once said, "You miss 100 percent of the shots you don't take." I've noticed that many of the most accomplished people are actually flattered by your interest and are happy to chat. They are as likely to be disarmed by a warm, confident greeting as the next person. Keith Ferrazzi credits his father, a steelworker, for setting a fearless example. Dad approached the CEO of his company to introduce little Keith, a move that led to an Ivy League education for his son. He believed "audacity was often the only thing that separated two equally talented men and their job titles."[60] It became second nature to Keith to approach anyone who interested him. We don't have the magic Ferrazzi wand that will put you at perfect ease the next time you have the chance to network with a great, but it's worth the discomfort to go for it.

BE SOMEONE BIG PEOPLE WON'T BLOW OFF.

If you want to hold your own in conversations with virtually anyone, be someone people want to talk to. Interesting people have areas of intense interest and a point of view. They put a stake in the ground and become known for it, often increasing their visibility and appeal by blogging, speaking and writing articles. You could say they develop their own brand. Janet and I became a brand that's known for mentoring. We have something to say that we're passionate about, and it led directly to the next act after our CCO jobs; Swim is grounded in decades of helping people move up the ladder. Sean Moffitt advises that you travel as much as you can, be curious, be vocal and don't shy away from sharing your opinions on things that matter to you. Sharon MacLeod goes further by recommending you make damn sure that when you're going to meet a person who's important, you have something to say that reflects an understanding of who you're talking to. She said, "At first, seated next to [Unilever CEO] Paul Polman at dinner, I was a deaf-mute." She does her homework now; she knows something about their interests and what might be a burning issue for them at the moment. "A John LeBoutillier [president of Unilever Canada] may spend a week studying before an important visitor arrives." She also thinks through what she wants to get out of the exchange and acts accordingly. "I've noticed the most successful women are very clear and concise. They're focused if they want something out of the exchange; maybe there are three points they really want to register." Sharon goes so far as to say that if you're talking with a man, be aware that most men have little patience with verbose women. "Men don't respond well to women who talk a lot—seventeen things with no focus makes for an uninteresting conversation and you won't be remembered." On the flip side, she thinks women are exceptionally good at putting people at ease in conversation and often carry the day over the man in the group because of it.

LISTEN.

As important as it is to have something interesting to talk about as you approach someone you want to meet, if you really want to connect, it's equally helpful to know when to shut up. Shutting up is not my forte, and it was a good day when I met Claire Hassid, a marketing planner based in New York. Listening skills came up as we compared notes on the qualities of influential people. Claire said I'm not the only one; most people are way better at talking than listening, and it's amazing that good listening is so undervalued, considering it's a common thread among the most powerful, connected people. Think Bill Clinton, the poster boy for listening. Good listening is one of his most marked traits, a big part of his appeal. He makes the speaker feel like the only person in the crowd. Bill's eye contact and body language reinforce that he's engaged in what he's hearing, and he leaves the speaker feeling that what they said mattered to him. As Claire puts it, listening is a gift you give the speaker.

Good listening is so overlooked as a powerful way to connect with people, that we frequently put focus on it in our leadership training. Before silently protesting that you're a good listener, maybe even known for it, take this test: have you ever been thinking about your response to the speaker as they're still sharing their point of view? When Claire told me the brain can't multitask the way you think it can, it made sense. If you're thinking about something else while someone is talking, you're missing information. And furthermore, your inattention tends to be easily seen by the speaker. You lose them when they realize you're not focused. One of the top barriers to strong connections with others is the lousy feeling of not being heard. This is true for co-workers, employees, your boss, your kids, and certainly anyone you're hoping to begin a relationship with. The next time you hope to make a good first impression, remember it's human to be drawn to people who make us feel heard. You'll be remembered for not only what you said, but what you didn't say. And you're more likely to be liked—the price of entry in successful networking.

MIRROR, MIRROR, THE PERSON STANDING BY THE WALL.

Mick Ebeling notes that everyone from heads of state to long-married couples "mirror," consciously or unconsciously. It's a deeply human trait to behave like the person you're communicating with, and it can help the would-be networker connect in what Mick calls the "micro-relationship that's possible in any conversation." Simply put, the psychologists tell us that when you slow down your cadence to the speed of the person you're talking with, or adopt their body language, eye movements, breathing or way of speaking, you put them at ease and they are more open to what you're saying. Mirroring is about awareness of who you're speaking to, being attuned to them. It shows real interest and respect. In long-standing or close family relationships, it happens naturally. But you can do it with more conscious effort and get the bene-fits. Mick's big watch-out: "Intent is everything. Approaching a person with genuine curiosity and interest is mandatory. You need to mirror emotionally and energetically, not just physically. You don't want to be a chimp making gestures."

DON'T BE USING THOSE FEMININE WILES.

Sean Moffitt noted with some dismay that the youngest business-women sometimes throw flirtation into the networking formula. If that influential man wants to help you based on a wink, you're on a slippery slope. Impress with your brains, wit, common interests and ambition. The suggestion of sex? We'll leave it at no good can come of this.

Dr. Ivan Misner, another co-author of *Business Networking and Sex (Not What You Think)* says women should be more mindful about what they wear to business events and how "provocative" their LinkedIn and Facebook profile pictures might be. His red flag, he told *Forbes*: don't look like a stereotype.

FACEBOOK CAN'T BEAT FACE TIME.

Could anything be more of a boon to networking than social networks? Humans have never been so easily connected with so many, but social networks have their limitations as a platform for dialogue and fostering real relationships. People like Keith and Sean go old-school for their most important conversations: email, phone calls and face time are still the best possible way to connect.

GET ORGANIZED.

You may find that your list of connections grows in a wonderfully organic way the more you network. But these connections can fade away when the busy person doesn't keep up. Dr. Misner said that his small business survey showed it pays to keep records and contacts organized to make it easy to stay on top of network communications. "Consistently, people who had systems in place did better whether they were men or women."[61]

SAY YES TO EVENTS, WITH CARE.

I don't need to tell you there's only so much of you to go around; of course you can't seize on every possible chance to meet great people. By asking myself what I really stand to get from conferences and events, I don't piss away energy on the wrong things. For me, saying yes to an invitation to participate in a weekend workshop held by Cape Farewell was a no-brainer. The group included impressive names from music, science, politics, art and comedy. We were unified by deep concern about climate change, and became a sort of think tank focused on making a dent in public awareness and on inspiring action. I felt honored to join the diverse group, and since then, spirited collaboration has led to provocative ideas. At the risk of sounding crass, yes, it also meant valuable new relationships. Diversity, by the way, is a great quality in any network. Homogenous groups tend to have a narrower perspective and same-y ideas.

IT'S NEVER TOO EARLY.

Coach your shy daughters (and sons, and not-shy daughters and sons) to put themselves out there as part of making their way into good jobs. In her final year of high school, my daughter, Lily, (who self-identifies as an introvert) knew she wanted to have a career in gaming animation. The wonderful Dex Deboree, an executive producer at an animation company in New York at the time, offered to connect me to a very senior person at Starz Animation in Toronto. He said, "I bet you could get Lily in there for a tour." Sure enough, we walked in their doors not long after, and after meeting Dex's friend, who spent quite a bit of time asking Lily about her views on the best games, we had a two-hour tour, accompanied by Jason McKenzie, the training manager. Lily's eyes were popping out of her head as we passed artists creating scenes for the latest Disney film. Over and over, she was able to ask questions of the specialists around her, and we ended our time in a boardroom with their head animator ready to take her questions on what he looks for in his hires. When we left, Jason aimed for a memorable moment. "Lily, you're here today because of networking. Your mom got you in here. Take notes; you'll get the job in huge part not because of talent or dedication. Start networking now. It's a fundamental."

It's time we flipped the cliché of networking on its head. You don't need to do it like the old boys. Shift your mental picture of it from talking to listening; from schmoozing and phony, to giving and authentic; from something you do, to a way of being that's generous and positive; from a distasteful man's game, to an approach to others that leads to rewarding friendships and new experiences; and, most definitely, from optional to mandatory.

To win, you have to play the game.

C lose your eyes for just a minute and picture a group of people sitting around a long table. The room is friendly enough but also a little tense. Some people are scanning the faces at the table. Others are concentrating on the information that's emerging in dribs and drabs. They speak in turn. Everyone is wondering who really holds the cards.

You've been there a thousand times, right? We've all been around that table. Oh, but wait. I wasn't talking about a boardroom; I was describing the rank beginner poker table I sat at with a bunch of other women on a chilly Friday night in November. The game was Texas Hold 'Em and, beyond my failure to fully grasp the difference between the Big Blind and Small Blind, the thing that struck me is how much poker is a metaphor for business: subtext, negotiation, bluffing, guessing and anticipation, advantage.

Not many women play poker, so the men around the table assume the lone woman will give it all away on her face, with a roll of her eyes, a sigh, a shake of her head. They expect that her decision making will be slow or timid, her bets conservative. They assume that she won't be clued in to all the different players and how the game needs to change depending on who is seated where at the table. Sound familiar? Yes, everything we're expected to blow in a game of poker, we're expected to blow in the game of business.

We've all heard about "the game." It's baked into business-speak: "I'm in the insurance game." "I'm in the ad game." It's in how businessmen size each other up—on the golf course or at a weekly game of hoops. It demands a certain bravado: no pain, no gain; mine is biggest; and I'm the decider. What it doesn't look for is authenticity. So many women respond by repressing their natural instincts, keeping their emotions in check and trying to pull on the ill-fitting "one of the guys" uniform to succeed.

Is this the only way? We don't think so. We're with Tess McGill from the 1980s movie *Working Girl*, who was definitely not going to work her butt off and get nowhere by sticking to rules she had nothing to do with creating.

Yes, business is a game, but we believe that women can redefine the rules, make it into an enlightened game, if you will. We each have to figure out how to play on our own terms.

Do the right thing

I was a fledgling writer at a time when cigarettes and advertising went together like fish and chips, Batman and Robin, Scotch and rocks. The Marlboro Man had been a celebrity for thirty years. Camel's Joe Camel was in his heyday. The sexy Virginia Slims women had come a long way, baby. And Ogilvy had a massive cigarette account. It seemed glamorous with big budgets, scripts that began with the words, "Open on palm tree . . . " People begged, bribed and stole for the chance to be involved. I'd been at Ogilvy about a year, when our boss, Tony Houghton, told me he wanted me to work on the account. I'd always wanted to work on a high-profile brand and here was my big chance. Except—it was cigarettes. Really not my deal. I didn't smoke. Never had. My chain-smoking parents had long since seen to that.

Clueless kid that I was, I told Tony that I couldn't *pahhhsibly* take the assignment. He was a friendly guy, warm, with a dry English sense of humor—he'd once been a writer for the great comic actor Peter Sellers, the Pink Panther himself. I figured a guy like that would let me off the hook.

He raised an eyebrow and said, "You understand that I could fire you for that?"

GULP. I did *not* see that coming. That wasn't part of my script. I took a deep breath, searching for the right reply.

"Ummm . . . well . . . I hope you won't," I said. "This office is full of smokers. There are ten people who'd do a way better job than me." Oh yeah. I had him.

"And do you also understand that even if you don't work on the account, cigarettes still pay your salary?"

BIGGER GULP. I didn't know that either. I had no idea how the "business of advertising" worked. It doesn't take a genius to figure out that when you're at the bottom of the heap, you're supposed to do what you're told, but I'd said no before working that part out. All I knew was that I couldn't tell a good story about a pack of cigarettes. In turning down the project, I'd broken an unspoken code I didn't even know existed.

When I said no to cigarettes, I had no idea that I was putting my job on the line. (Lucky for me, I had a boss who cut me some slack and let me keep my job and my social conscience.) I wasn't a card-carrying, placard-waving, anti-smoking radical. I just couldn't bring myself to tell others to do it, and naively, I said so without imagining a downside. I'd never had any "how to behave in business" education. No one in my family had ever worked for "the man." My own brief work history—at the dry cleaners in high school, teaching French and English to Spanish kids after university, and a brief stint writing catalogue copy—wasn't much in the way of prep for the "real world." The only businessmen I'd ever known were my meteorologist dad's radio station colleagues and the bar mitzvah DJs who worked for my mom's roving DJ company. Not exactly Fortune 500. So I was ill equipped for the uniform: no poker face, no poker feelings.

Don't be a naive newbie

Of course, not everyone is as naive as I was when I started. Women like Martine get that work is a game, and they play along—even though it can cost them emotionally to do it. Martine works on the trading floor of a large investment bank; she's one of a small group of women among three hundred men. She's on the floor from 6:30 in the morning till 5:30 in the afternoon, without a lunch break. Co-op students fetch her coffee and bring her food, even if they have to go to five different places to find the perfect sandwich. Heck, they'd pee for her if they could.

Martine is twenty-nine, with a pixie cut, the face of an angel and a manner to match, but the girl who would have described herself as shy five years earlier said, "On the floor, I'm tough, and I'm out there to eat their lunch."

"It's a weird culture. It's a *good* thing when somebody makes fun of you. Means you're accepted. And when I say making fun, it's not just a few cracks. For instance, you're trying to do a trade or trying to find information for your boss, and someone says, 'Oh Martine, that took way too long. What the f*** are you doing? You should do this thing in three seconds or you're never going to get hired,' or, 'Who have you hooked up with on the floor,' all day long. They call it chirping. I can chirp back to them, but you have to know how, not be too aggressive, because they rule. You have to let it roll off you. Sometimes it hurts my feelings, but men don't want to hear about it. You have to develop a pretty hard shell. I try to make sure to leave it at the office, but it doesn't always go that way."

I admire Martine's thick skin, and I know that for her, toughening up and adapting to the workplace culture was a necessary survival skill. But many women opt out of the business world because they're not willing to work the way the game seems to demand. Maybe it's taking too much of a toll on their home lives. Maybe they can't reconcile what their companies expect with who they are. In the past, opting out was just that. Now it can be a new way to succeed, as so many of these women are inventing their own futures as tremendous entrepreneurs. The number of women-owned firms in the United States increased by 59 percent over the last fifteen years,[62] and one in five global start-ups is now women-led.[63] Maybe they should be our role models, because one of the reasons women are such kickass entrepreneurs is that they operate by their own rules, which include shocking things like frankness, being yourself, being your own best cheerleader and even learning to love your inexperience. Mine turned out to be my best friend.

Finding joy in a career is critical. Martine puts up with the frat house on the trading floor because she loves the work, but she draws a line: Martine brings a woman's point of view to the table.

McKinsey's continuous Centered Leadership study tells us that "more than men, [many] women prize the opportunity to pour their energies into making a difference and working closely with colleagues. Women don't want to trade that joy for what they fear will be energy-draining meetings and corporate politics at the next management echelon."[64] In other words, many women would rather not have a bigger job if it's only about delivering on the bottom line. Most women are looking for meaning in the work they do and that affects the career choices they make. They're not just looking for the win.

Authenticity is the new black

Think about the businesspeople you admire most. Are they great at their jobs? Are they the ones who land the biggest deals, or the ones who land big deals and teach others their secrets? Do your best bosses raise the company's stock or do they raise the stock and inspire the people with a mission? For a few years, Nancy and I worked for Brian Fetherstonhaugh, a CEO who not only led a healthy organization but knew the names of all 253 employees and most of their kids. He wore tracks in the hallway carpets as he dropped in for chats, asked after vacations and spouses and children's birthdays. He kept a harmonica in his pocket and pulled it out whenever the mood struck, even if he was in a client meeting or new business pitch. The whole staff turned up for "town halls" where everyone heard where we were headed and how we were doing getting there. From mailroom guy to managing director, everyone felt that they were contributing to a common goal. Brian left Canada over fifteen years ago, but people still talk about him; some who never met him feel as if they have. He wanted his company to be both the best in the network and a happy, humane place. Brian led with his humanity on his sleeve and his real self on display.

Even as your authenticity benefits you and the group around you, it can appear to come with personal risk. Sharon MacLeod of Unilever realized that after a long, long slog of being understaffed and overworked, her normally upbeat team was down and discouraged. She asked the head of the employee assistance program to spend an hour with every member of her team of forty or so. She wanted to know what was working for them, what wasn't, what they liked about her and her boss, and what they didn't. Talk about opening a can of worms. When the report came, it had many positives, but it was also full of the negative feelings of exhausted people. Sharon told her boss that they had to share it wholesale—undoctored, unedited, unshielded by HR. She called a meeting of her entire staff. As she stood in front of her group, Sharon told them that she was there to apologize. She said it was one of the hardest days of her career, because it was the day she had to tell them that she knew in full color how she'd let them down. She said, "I take full responsibility for the ways in which I've failed you. I'm standing here in front of you and in front of my boss to talk about it. I know you don't always feel like you can speak your mind, but I want you to know that if I can do this in front of you and in front of my boss, you can talk freely too."

That level of vulnerability is foreign to most people in leadership roles. Yet allowing people to meet the real you is one of the less examined hallmarks of great leadership. If there had been a love meter in the room, the arrow would've whipped straight to eleven. Those people would have followed her anywhere. That moment of extreme openness was also a moment of power, the kind that draws people to you rather than pushes them away. Isn't that what every leader wants? And it came from Sharon just deciding to change the game and let them see her humanity.

Get better at being you

At the time I started copywriting, there were few ways to learn the skill other than on the job. I lucked into my first job, my employment based on little more than "she seems like a nice girl and she can string a sentence." I knew nothing about advertising, clients or selling, or even how to write an ad. So I mimicked. I styled myself after the writers I admired. I studied the ad books and borrowed the tone of the work I saw there. I went to early-morning account-management training programs to learn the language: Nielsen ratings, ROI, reach and frequency. After all, wouldn't I need to say those words myself to be credible?

Then there was the morning that I found myself telling my client that I'd spent the night before in the hospital getting stitches put into my three-year-old's lip, and that while we were waiting, I'd thoughtlessly let him sip my lemonade, careless young mama that I was. And in turn, she let me in on her mothering missteps, inadvertently establishing a connection we hadn't had before. As

I opened up my life to them, many of my clients responded with theirs. Bonds began to form. Little kernels of trust grew because we'd developed an unspoken pact to be human with each other. If you'd told me that my bad mom stories were the secret to making my clients more inclined to buy my ideas, I would've checked your forehead for a high fever. Today, if you Google "authenticity + business," you'll find 145 million entries telling you that it's the most important business tool since the laser pointer. Back then, just choosing to be myself in the room changed everything, whereas trying to play the game hadn't served me in the least.

Live with the consequences

Choosing to be yourself will not guarantee you a VIP pass to the happy land of cotton candy and free pedicures. As I learned when I said no to the cigarette campaign, taking a position can be polarizing. People might not agree with you. They might not even want to work with you.

Every business has its status quo, those well-known practices that everyone understands and tacitly agrees to. In advertising, one of them is using consumer research to judge creative ideas. Ad people put weeks of energy, tons of money, years of combined experience and masses of creativity into every project. Then we put that creative work into the hands of ten or twenty "regular" people who will pronounce on it for fifty bucks and free sandwiches. Nancy and I have never been fans. And we said so, in no uncertain terms, in the first big speech of our career, "If You're in the Middle of the Road, You're Going to Get Run Over." There were several hundred people in the room, mostly marketers and researchers. We weren't just rocking the boat, we were capsizing it. That speech made us heroes in some people's eyes, zeroes in others'. (Even seven years later, our CEO came to my office to tell me that a new client didn't want us involved in a project because we'd gone on record with that opinion years earlier.) We couldn't be sure how things would land when we shared our controversial perspective with the very people we were challenging that day. It certainly established that we had a point of view.

Over the years, Nancy and I became known as people who would tell the truth as we saw it, even if what we had to say wasn't well received. That frankness built trust, and it usually served everyone well, even on those painful occasions when we had to fire people.

In the standard game, firing is a brutal, cold affair. In a screenplay, the scene would go like this: A guy is asked to come to his boss's office. He has a bad feeling. He looks in the door. Someone he's never seen before is there too. His boss introduces him to "Roger, from HR." The guy's heart starts to race. "Please, sit," says Roger. The boss says nothing. "Today will be your last day," says Roger. The shocked guy looks at his boss, who doesn't look at him, doesn't speak. The boss gets up and leaves the room. The guy looks at Roger, starts to speak. Roger says, "Someone is packing up your office. We'll have your things sent to your home."

Except it wasn't a screenplay. It was what a former employee told me when he called for advice just after being sacked by the agency where he worked. I was staggered by the unfeeling behavior of his boss. What I didn't know then was that this is typical of the way many organizations handle difficult employee issues: it's impersonal, cold and takes the pressure off the decision maker. Leaving it up to HR to swing the axe keeps emotions at bay and maybe lessens the likelihood of a lawsuit. But Nancy and I always felt that we needed to look a person in the eye if we had bad news. They deserved their chance to say whatever they needed to say. The way we saw it was that we were talking about people's lives. We had various reasons to let people go: hiring mistakes, bad fit, budget cuts. It was always different, but we always handled it the same way. Very few of those people have held it against us, because we heard them out. We treated them how we would want to be treated.

Laura Formusa, former CEO of Hydro One, offered this gem at a *Globe and Mail* women's forum: "Two things I always say: work hard and be yourself. You can't compromise on either one of those things. And I know 'be yourself' sounds like a really soft thing. But it is not. You can tell a fake from a mile away. There's something about authenticity. Don't change yourself to suit other people. It's your personality. It's your values. You have to be true to them."[65]

Why is being yourself so darned hard?

If bringing our real selves to work is a good idea, what makes it so tough to do? For one thing, it can mean having to stick your neck out or raise your hand or put down your foot in a way that might put the limb at risk. That, in turn, could mean bad client meetings or conflict with bosses. But it also means that people always know where you stand, which is usually appreciated in the long run, if not the short.

Sharon MacLeod believed the game didn't matter, until she got the review that said, "Sharon is starting to understand politics, but she's naive." She wasn't trying hard enough to get the attention of her boss; she wasn't making herself visible—critical in a multinational—and she wasn't sharing enough of her output with the company. Sharon was doing what women do: being a good girl who did a good job and waiting for her bosses to notice. That's how it works in a meritocracy, right? "It's *not* a meritocracy." Ahh. She took courses, talked to mentors to better understand the lay of the land. She started to read the signals, to figure out when, how and to whom she should wave the flag of her accomplishments. Her view changed: women don't have to play the game, per se, but it helps to know which game you're not playing and then take your own informed choices forward. For Sharon, that included bringing warmth into chilly boardrooms, choosing hugging over handshakes and putting special focus on helping other women hurtle over the obstacles in their way. As the longtime Canadian lead on Dove's progressive, mission-based Campaign for Real Beauty, Sharon set her goal further than just selling more bars of soap or bottles of body wash. "When I work on Dove, it's part of who I am as a person."[66] Once she understood the rules, she played her own way.

Learn the dialect

When Daryl Aitken, Judy Elder and Katie Zemla decided to get involved in their office fantasy baseball pool, they did it just for fun. What were all those guys on about anyway? They seemed to be having a great time and the women wanted in on the action. They knew nothing about baseball, except that Toronto had a good team a couple of times a century and that the World Series only includes North America.

Stats junkie Daryl pored over the sports pages, listened to the broadcasts, followed the tables. Kind of like Jonah Hill in *Moneyball*, she did the research, and to everyone's shock, the women won—not just the pot, but status. Suddenly, they were included in different kinds of conversations; men talked to them in the elevator about— you guessed it—sports, which created a new sense of connection. It created a relationship that hadn't existed.

The same insight underpins The Gal's Got Game, Lally Rementilla's online service that delivers just enough sports info to women's inboxes daily to allow them to invite themselves into any conversation they choose.

Lally, vice president of finance and administration at logistics software company Nulogy Corporation, has had an exceptional track record of profitably growing companies like Lucent Technologies Canada, Lavalife and now Nulogy. But as she confessed to her husband, she needed a new challenge. She was looking for something that would help women advance in the work world, but it needed to be different from anything else out there—something that would give women an edge. She and her friend Rekha Shah were with their daughters on a playdate as Lally talked about it.

"I know exactly what to do. I've known for four years," Rekha said. "We need to help women understand sports." Rekha listened to the men in her workplace gather every Monday morning and rehash the games they'd played and the sports they'd watched over the weekend. She heard their excitement over the basketball, baseball, hockey and football that was to come that week. Rekha didn't speak that language. Her idea was to send out a daily email to tell women just enough of what was happening in sports that they could get in on the conversation if they wanted to. Sports is the great neutralizer, the ground that brings together the mailroom guy and the CEO. Why not women?

They worked to bring the idea to life in the slim window of spare time moms have. Rekha gave up driving to build in more time to read the sports news, books on golf, and *Sports Illustrated* on the subway. Lally developed the strategy, website and partnerships.

Lally led negotiations on a critical contract for Nulogy. The only woman in the room with an Italian, an American, a Brit and a Dutch guy, this Filipina-Canadian was about as close to an alien as they were likely to meet that day, and she knew she had to find some common ground. The FIFA World Cup was on. "I'd learned just enough about soccer." It broke the ice and created an instant connection. The contract was signed, and she gives a lot of credit to the game Europeans call "futbol." Today, The Gal's Got Game is a sports website that tells women exactly what they need to know, not too much, not too little. A stable of writers on golf, soccer, hockey, you name it, keeps the information coming. Their subscribers read it every day; their email boxes are full of thank-you notes from bankers, lawyers, consultants, accountants, women in private equity firms and large consumer goods companies, and women entrepreneurs who suddenly feel that they have an "in," an understanding of a language that was opaque to them.

Kathleen Warner, former COO of Startup America Partnership has worked in mostly male businesses. "I've never found it too challenging to be in a large group of guys, but there's an oddness nonetheless. There's authenticity in being who you are and knowing what you know, but the notion of knowing the language is a good one. I've worked in the financial sector, in law, entrepreneurship, the federal government and had to learn them all. You need to know the lingo of people you're spending time with, including men."

Bluff with the best

When Richard Branson came to speak at an advertising industry educational event in Toronto in 2010, he also signed on to judge a student competition for ideas to launch Virgin Mobile's RE*Generation campaign in Canada. Teams of students led by young ad agency professionals from several local shops had three frantic hours to answer Virgin's brief and email the solution to a committee. The top three presentations would be invited to make a five-minute "elevator" pitch to Branson, and the idea he chose would be made. *Tick. Tick. Tick.* The word came that the team mentored by Ogilvy people had been selected. The group had thirty minutes to get to a downtown location. But a blizzard slowed down the cabs. They arrived ten minutes late for their pitch time, swooping in just as the selection was being made between the other two agencies. Coby Shuman, *nouveau* mad man, all knife-creases and Windsor knot, was the head of Ogilvy's team. He pleaded for the chance to present the idea, citing the blizzard, taxis, only a few minutes late. No, said the committee.

Then Coby saw Branson come out of a small room and head for the elevator. Coby changed his focus. "Sir Richard, we were a few minutes late, thanks to Canadian weather, but you can see that we're all here and ready to share our winning idea. Your executives said we were too late, but here you still are. Please let us make a real elevator pitch. Let us ride down with you. In that time, I can show you why you're not being ambitious enough. Let us tell you how you can make a bigger impact on youth homelessness and be known as a social champion."

The room was watching. The media was filming as Branson held open the elevator door and said, "Come on in." Coby and the students all squeezed in as Coby turned their five-minute story into a sixty-second one. As the doors opened on the ground floor, Branson said, "If you'd arrived on time, yours would be the idea being made," and headed off to the airport.

Coby was young and brash and didn't hesitate for a second to fling himself in front of the world's boldest entrepreneur. Would you have done that? Would most women? I know that I wouldn't have. I'd have felt that I was imposing. I'd have decided that I'd missed my chance and I'd just have to suck it up. I suspect that most of us would've been more like me than like Coby.

But the reason for it may be different than you think. Maybe what stands between women and leaping into the elevator with Richard Branson is the same thing that causes them to refuse a compliment or to dismiss their success. It's astoundingly common among intelligent high achievers of both genders, but with a double scoop for women. It's called "imposter syndrome," and while both men and women experience it, women wear it for the world to see. *What if I'm found out? What if they discover I succeeded through luck?* If the game is about being Oz, the great and powerful, it's why we put so much energy into being Dorothy, the small and meek.[67] And it gets in the way of our authentic selves.

This book is full of highly accomplished, successful women by any objective measure, yet when I asked them about imposter syndrome, it was as if I'd stuck them with an electric cattle prod. A light went on in almost every eye. The need to confess was overwhelming. Not a single woman I spoke to said, "Imposter what?"

I know how they feel. I do a ton of public speaking and have for years—small audiences, large ones, students, company presidents, they're all the same to me. Each time out, it's as if it were the first—the butterflies, the sleepless nights, the out-of-body experience of it all. When I look really hard at the reason, it isn't stage fright. It's because part of me is always saying, "Why should they care what I think?" It has been the single biggest daily challenge that I have faced in my career.

When psychotherapist Kali Hewitt-Blackie was teaching psychology at the New School in Montreal, she wanted her students to better understand the grading process, so she had them grade themselves. Most of the boys gave themselves an easy A, while even the smartest girl was hard-pressed to give herself a B or even a C.

Why is it that so few high-achieving women feel entitled to their accomplishments? Why do so many of us feel that we don't deserve it? Owning it isn't where women excel.

My friend Margaret would often jokingly say, "I pretty much got my PhD by accident." Except she wasn't really joking. She really did feel she'd "lucked into a brilliant subject" and "had a good day" when she defended her thesis. Thank God, no one had noticed she didn't deserve it. An institution granted her degree, but that wasn't enough because she didn't feel it. Most of us grow up depending on validation for accomplishments to matter. A great report card is evidence of some kind of success, but a parent's excitement over that report card is the thing that makes it feel that it was worth doing. The validation gets a whole lot less as time goes on. No wonder we think we're frauds. Dr. Valerie Young, imposter syndrome expert and author of *The Secret Thoughts of Successful Women*, told *The Wall Street Journal* that "the places where women are apt to feel the most incompetent and illegitimate are in the public spheres of power and authority."[68] We're still new to the game and it shows.

Just as men don't let the need to be liked get in their way, they also don't wear their doubt on their sleeve. They don't publicize the fact they don't know how to do something; they just tell themselves they'll figure it out. We hesitate. We wait till we feel that we know enough to do the job. The judgments on us are harsher, so we want to get it right the first time; we miss opportunities and fail ourselves because we feel like imposters.

Being yourself is the best sleep aid

So what does it matter if we don't bring our true selves to the table? What happens when you stick to your knitting, behave like a "good girl," "toe the line," as my mother says? Maybe it all works out, but in the words of Pulitzer Prize–winning author Laurel Ulrich, "well-behaved women seldom make history." Good girls also don't get promoted, don't change anything, and don't get what they want. Geeta Sheker, director of the Initiative for Women in Business at the Rotman School, shared the view that men are promoted on potential and women on performance. If that's true, we need to make it possible for our bosses to see our potential and to know our true selves, and that doesn't happen by holding back or sitting on the sidelines.

What about when your true-to-you comes into conflict with other people's true-to-them, as it undoubtedly will? Sometimes, you'll wind up leaving where you work because you wake up with a knot in your stomach or in your conscience. Other times, things fall into place. You work through a problem in a more honest, effective way and the outcome serves everyone involved. Not only that, you develop a reputation as a thoughtful, challenging colleague.

When Jules sold her strategy company to a larger firm, she worked out a contract that gave her an earn-out based on the revenue of her company. She would build incremental revenue for them, and continue to operate as if independent. Within months of her joining, as they were doing their fiscal plans for the next year, the firm suddenly decided to change the deal: her earn-out would be based on the profitability of the whole organization. Jules had crafted her arrangement carefully because her confidence lay in what she could control. She wrote a long, legal-like letter reminding them of the details of the original agreement. There was no response. Weeks went by. Nothing. Then she got a call from management telling her that the firm was struggling and that she'd have to fire three people. But Jules's part of the company was doing just fine. She had three people on mat leave and way too much work to let anyone go. Besides, she could afford her staff. Every day for a week, the manager called to ask if she'd decided who would get the axe. Jules asked how much money they wanted from her company. The answer was "$200,000." "Fine. I quit," she said. She walked away from it all.

I cheered as Jules told me the end of the story. "It's a very female story," she said. "I've never told it to a man who didn't say, 'Are you crazy? Why didn't you sue them?'" But Jules thinks life is too short to be spent in negative energy and legal wrangling. She made the choice to withdraw her talent, skills and time; she wasn't interested in helping people like that become successful. She told them that she wouldn't sue them as long as they ignored the non-compete clause in the contract and gave her back the rights to all her clients. Instead of spending her energy fighting, she spent it building a new company.

Of course, you won't always get what you want even with "true to you" as your guiding light, but you'll sleep better. In general, people would prefer to make each other happy. Compromise can be reached, breakthrough can be made, and a client or co-worker or boss can hear your honest point of view, and you theirs. The key is to understand the game and know when you're not willing to play. We say, let your own values and judgment be your guide, even as you are picking your way through a world of foul balls and offsides. When we have spoken and acted authentically, there has sometimes been short-term, occasionally very acute, pain, but even as we stumbled through significant challenges with all the finesse of a pair of baby elephants, things usually worked out.

When we delivered our controversial research speech, we risked alienating our clients, their research partners and our own boss. When we changed the way Dove advertising was done, in some people's eyes, we risked hurting the brand. But when we didn't stand up for something we believed in, we hurt ourselves. The things you should have done chew on your conscience a lot longer than they would if you'd just gone ahead and done them and seen what happened.

Years ago, we went to an Ogilvy creative directors' gathering where the speaker was Malcolm McLaren, artist, fashion designer and manager of the Sex Pistols. His mission in life was to be a "magnificent failure," in other words, someone who experimented constantly without regard for consequences. "Success is so boring," he said to us. He described his first store, where he refused to sell anything, and the next one, which was housed below street level so the clientele were expected to jump down onto a muddy floor to get in. His bondage pants had two legs sewn together, so you could buy them, but you couldn't use them. To his chagrin, his approach brought him success after success. Malcolm's role was to inspire us with his individuality and bravery and his commitment to being himself. He said, "You can live a life that's authentic or a life that's karaoke." We've tried very hard not to be karaoke.

Today, with easy access to information, people's growing mistrust of corporations, and their growing trust of peer networks and even strangers, the business climate has changed significantly. Whatever "trust" meant in the past, it's taken on tremendous importance in the present, and people are more inclined to put their faith in those who don't play games, who strike them as "for real."

Forever burned in my brain is the day David Rutherford, Ogilvy Toronto's former vice-chair, said to me, "You'd be good at this job if you didn't wear your face on your face." We were walking down the hall toward the creative department after a meeting where I might have rolled my eyes once too often. New to leadership, I took instant offense. He made the point that it was good that I was "me," but that I needed to learn to be more aware of what my face was saying. My transparency has mostly been a good thing, but David was right, of course, about the big downside of someone walking around all snarly-faced because of a bad day. That said, one of the big reasons people felt so comfortable with me was they felt that my emotional self was available to them. They could literally see how I felt; they had access to my heart self, not just my head self. I believe that "wearing my face on my face" is one of the reasons I was good at my senior jobs.

Nancy and I put our foot in it countless times. Occasionally, we blew it off. But overall, being exactly ourselves has been a great strategy. Being up front about where we stand has served us in the long run. It's meant conflict, discomfort, occasional brief catastrophe (I've been fired twice)—but it's usually worked out. No strong leader is a big fake.

There is no game if there are no players. Women can bring their gutsy, open-minded, emotionally present, intuitive selves to work every day, along with their intelligence, hard work and talent. Kermit the wise frog says it isn't easy being green. Truthfully, it's not always easy to be authentic, but it's better than the alternative, and it pays you back, with interest.

Ambition is a straight line to the top.

My neighbor Victoria shared a vision of an ambitious life with me. It's a vision she learned at the knee of her grandmother Alessandra, who had been a successful journalist, editor and mother of three, and who ultimately wound up living on Lago di Como, not far from George Clooney's. Go, Granny, go.

Alessandra described her life to her granddaughter this way: "Women's lives don't follow a straight line, especially if they have children. I never wanted to just get from here to there. It wasn't interesting to me. I jumped from lily pad to lily pad, sometimes a smaller one, sometimes a bigger one depending on what I wanted in my life at that time."

Lily pad to lily pad—I love that. Not the ladder straight up through the clouds most of us picture when we think about how careers progress, but a zigzag journey with room for life, experience and the opportunity for surprise. Alessandra's notions of success and ambition are sprawling and generous. And remarkably, her metaphor lends an image to the views of so many of the women we spoke to while writing this book. Even though we see them as the picture of accomplishment, they tended to back away from answering how they'd describe the role of ambition in their own success. Not because they weren't reaching and striving, but because they didn't like the word: the old definition didn't work for them.

Words have their own baggage, their own legacy. We understand success and ambition according to a male-centric definition. While "top title, most power" has been the goal for decades, the brass ring these women reached for was bigger and richer. Their definition of "making it" looked more like a desire for authenticity, the chance to do work that meant something to them, and the desire for an abundant life, not merely dying with the most toys.

Dictionaries tell us that ambition is the "ardent desire for rank, fame, and power" (*The Merriam-Webster Dictionary*) or the pursuit of "success, wealth and fame" (*Oxford English Dictionary*). "Ardent desire" suggests a passionate, laser-focused journey to a specific end—"rank, fame, power, wealth"—arrived at with at least a soupçon of aggression and a dash of arrogance. The word continues to smack of the need to be "the king of the castle," not the crown most women are after.

My career was no straight-line ladder climb from bottom to top.

I was in advertising and out of it. I did different jobs when I was out—teaching, writing for a kids' magazine, singing in a bar band. Looking back, I'd describe my ambition as the desire to have what I wanted professionally, without giving up what I loved, and it's meant making choices, compromises, moving slower at certain times and faster at others. And that's worked for me.

Don't be afraid to zigzag

For American Express's Denise Pickett, ambition looked like new experiences. "I've never been hungry to progress, only hungry to learn. I have to be learning and gaining skills to be happy. There are people whose advice would always be 'keep your eyes on the prize.' Mine would be 'learn everything you can, try everything you can, show you're willing, get results' and the rest follows."

The rest follows. What kind of ambitious businessperson says that? The accepted wisdom is that you need to visualize an absolute goal such as "I want to be a CEO by age thirty" or "I want to run the biggest sales territory in the country before the end of the year," then draw the line backward through the steps you need to take to get there—a straight line, the best and only way to get from A to B. But what if the accepted wisdom doesn't work for you? Can't there be another way? Several other ways? A straight line is what makes us afraid to have kids; if we step off the path, we'll never get back on. We say yes if we're offered a promotion, even if it's not right for us. What if we don't get another chance?

Take heart. It doesn't have to be that black and white. Denise turned down opportunities if she thought they'd compromise her personal life too much. She said no to a promotion when her third son was eighteen months old. When her male leader called her to ask why she'd declined, she said she couldn't commit to living on an airplane at that moment in her life. She also told him she hoped it wouldn't have a negative impact on her career. It hasn't.

But notice something: when Denise tipped the scales firmly toward her personal life, she also dropped a pebble into the other pan by letting her leader know that her career was important to her. I believe the fact that she told him she hoped she wouldn't suffer for it is part of why she didn't suffer for it. When Sabrina Geremia went to talk to Google about her future while she was on mat leave, she let them know that her career was critical to her. Her asking what they needed from her when she came back, rather than telling them what she expected from them, opened new doors. For almost a year, her twins were the whole deal. The new job she took when she came back became a surprising fast track to managing director. You never know when stepping off the ladder might open up a lily pad you hadn't seen.

Kathleen Warner spent the last twenty-five years focused on having the life she wanted, with kids *and* ambition. Her winding road has taken her from law to finance, to a congressman's office to COO of Startup America Partnership. A willingness to ebb and flow, a husband who was ready to tag-team from the beginning, and what Kathleen calls integration and alchemy have all come together to enable her lifelong ambition to have an impact in the world. Her daughter, who used to ask why her mom couldn't be a waitress in a diner, spoke at graduation and said, "My mother is a force and an inspiration to pursue your passions and dreams."

Like Denise and Sabrina, Kathleen has defined her own way of working to give herself the biggest canvas possible. "Women need to own and celebrate their successes and accomplishments and affirmatively go after projects, promotions and money, even, maybe especially, if it feels uncomfortable. This can be addressed in part by those of us who have had non-linear career paths and our fair share of both failure and success standing up, being visible and vocal, and also giving back through mentoring and advising." It's hard for women to aspire to be like role models if there are none to be seen.

Be the architect of your fulfillment

Nancy and I had been content—no, joyful—in our one-below-the-top job for five years, so much so that we'd said "a thousand times no" to the big title each time it was put in front of us. We'd invested a lot of years in not wanting to run anything. Who needed it? Our bosses never seemed especially happy. They seldom went home. It always looked like a compromise too far, which is why when we made the jump, we did it together.

Hold the phone, sister. What do you mean together? What kind of ambition is that? Isn't success all about winning? About being number one? Steve Landsberg, the boss we'd eventually replace, would often say to us, "It isn't about winning. It's about getting what you want." Winning per se doesn't need to be the goal. What drives you? What vision do you have for your life? For us, Steve's words have been words to live by.

We needed to create the conditions that would give us the greatest chance not just of career success but also of happiness. We didn't want to be phone-it-in moms or phone-it-in creative directors, or in my case, a phone-it-in wife. We had to stop letting our careers happen to us and start designing the life we wanted, like Bonnie Wan did.

Bonnie was an über-successful brand strategist at a San Francisco marketing firm in 2007. It was a position and pay scale she'd spent years building through logging the hours, pulling the all-nighters, crisscrossing the country. Only she didn't feel successful. She felt like a failure.

Picture Bonnie sitting in the living room at her parent's house, where she always stayed when she was in L.A. on business. She was on her laptop, trying to work, but all she could think about was her family, hundreds of miles away in San Francisco. She was thinking about how her husband, Chip, had put their kids—ages three and one—to bed single-handedly. Again. Bonnie was in agony—you know it, that piercing, gut-wrenching pain you feel when your life is totally off-kilter and the things you value most are the things you have the least time for.

Even when she was in San Francisco, she barely saw her family. She left for work before breakfast and felt lucky on the nights she got home for bedtime. She traveled several times a month. In that moment in L.A., she felt a huge, internal crisis bubble up inside her. "I was not the wife I had committed to being when we got married. I was certainly not the parent I had signed up to be." She'd been feeling it for months but hadn't acknowledged her struggle until that night. So she opened a new document on her computer and started writing. Only this time it wasn't a brand strategy document. It was a vision for what she wanted her life to be.

When she was finished, she emailed the document to her husband, Chip. He texted her back immediately: YES.

Over the next two years, Bonnie and Chip began a drastic redesign of their life. They bought a house in Portland, where the cost of living was lower and the public schools were excellent, and the family could afford to have Chip stay at home full-time. Bonnie negotiated a new deal at work that would allow her to work four days a week—one of them from home—and commute to San Francisco for two days a week. *Commute to San Francisco two days a week?* Yes, and today she's able to spend more time than ever with her family, which now includes four children. Her focus is on leadership training and development. As compared to the traditional notion of ambition—one foot in front of the other, rung by rung, upward—Bonnie's is a lateral move perhaps, but one that fulfills her the way her brand strategy job used to. What's most important for Bonnie is that she's living the life she wrote about on that L.A. night six years ago.

I love Bonnie's story because it gets at the heart of what ambition really can be—when we have the courage to own the word. Ambition becomes the creative drive inside that pushes us to design and live the lives that *we* really want, not the lives or careers we're supposed to want, based on a workplace dominated by a set of rules that worked for men.

At age sixteen, Joanne Thomas Yaccato wanted to work in service to the world at large, whatever that meant. The accidental entrepreneur-writer and president of the Thomas Yaccato Group, who started off educating women about money, and financial institutions about women, now travels the world as senior international gender finance advisor to the World Bank. She finds that women around the globe are increasingly moving into entrepreneurship to achieve their ambitions. Her own ambition led her to work on behalf of women and, like so many others in this book, create a life that has room for family and extraordinary adventure. As a young woman, she wouldn't have been able to dream up the work she does now, because nothing like it existed. "I really had to think about my ambition. I had to weigh what I was getting from the traditional male model of status and money against what I was getting from this work. This isn't about status at all. I let go of all of that because international development doesn't allow for it. I'm less of a perfectionist now, because you have to be. I don't overplan things. I show up and I'm flexible and aware. I operate on a kind of controlled rolling-with-it model."

"But you were trapped in Taksim Square during the uprising in Turkey," I said.

"Yeah—that's the fun of it," she said excitedly. "You never know what's going to happen. For instance, I went to Oman to do a megaproject. Eight large focus groups of women, all in abayas. One group turned out to be Oman's first woman architect, first female civil engineer, first woman to climb Mount Kilimanjaro. As one of them said, you'd never have guessed it because of these robes." Women's ambition is taking off everywhere. Creating your own rules for living is causing women to walk away from conventional businesses and business models and start their own, where their own rules apply and their own ambition is in charge.

Ambition isn't just about personal achievement. Denise was ambitious for her family to have a new experience, and they were equally so for her. Joanne was ambitious for women's financial freedom, Kathleen to see more women lead, and Kate James for the next generation. Ambition isn't an end in itself, so perhaps if you're still a little uneasy with the word, it would help to think about what you're ambitious *for*.

The women in this book have all stretched and reached. Some were ambitious out of the womb, others not till much later. They often didn't adhere to the rules that were written before they got there, because those rules weren't designed for them. Their paths were frequently crooked and creative.

Will you choose the ladder or the lily pads? A ladder is a fine, sturdy means of climbing. If you choose the lily pads, maybe you'll find they suit you better—and jumping has more joy to it.

Darling, you can do both (and then some)

So where do we go from here? What's in store for you, for our gender, as we tap our fingers while the "system" catches up to what we have to offer?

As more women land in high places, more hands will be held out to the ones coming up behind them. Surely the institutions are bound to change when the balance shifts a little more. The pendulum is creaking the other way, albeit far too slowly; the 2013 Catalyst report is filled with far too much same old, same old. Unconscious bias is alive and well. New research continues to point to the fact that women grads earn dramatically less than men. And, frustratingly, while there are still too few women on boards and in senior roles, many C-suite men don't think it's a problem.[69] When men leave a job, they are still more likely to hand over the reins to other men. Business continues to think it's "more secure" with men running the show. No doubt, that's part of the reason that women's participation on boards and in corner offices has stayed virtually unchanged despite the influx of women into positions of greater responsibility. It's a blind devotion to "if it ain't broke, don't fix it." Yet it's unquestionably broke. What better time for change?

Happily, there are those who are determined to give women a

giant push. Official and unofficial quota systems are popping up throughout Europe, helping get women onto more boards, despite controversy and debate: "Women don't have the experience, the history, the respect. What if they're not good enough?" What *if* some less-than-perfect women do slip into these big opportunities? Well, there are plenty of imperfect men in the system already.

What difference can women make? Why does it matter that we have a greater say in how the future unfolds? Maybe some new ideas would bloom in the world. In their 2013 study on female leadership, Professors David Matsa and Amalia Miller noticed that Norway, the first country to implement a quota system, is seeing that boards with 40 percent women take into account the long-term not just the short. They give out fewer pink slips and are willing to take the short-term hit in order to keep their teams together, believing this will be of benefit in the future. Similar decisions were made in women-led organizations in the United States during the recession. On a practical level, hiring and training may well be more costly than downsizing, but Matsa and Miller's research also suggests that "female leaders may have different values relating to the workforce compared with men in the same position. For example, an earlier study of Swedish corporate board members found that women placed a higher premium on what are known as self-transcendent values, things like benevolence and universalism, and less on self-enhancement values, like achievement and power, than their male colleagues. These differences might make leaders more sensitive to the needs of their workers, and less likely to lay them off even when demand is low."[70]

John Gerzema and Michael D'Antonio's global leadership survey, featured in their great book *The Athena Doctrine: How Women (and the Men Who Think Like Them) Will Rule the Future*, strongly suggested that the qualities associated with women, such as flexibility, collaboration and long-term thinking, are widely desirable—even in countries we don't associate with female success. They point to examples all over the world of problems that seemed too big to solve, yet a female style of leadership led to unconventional, highly effective solutions, from navigating Iceland through financial collapse to fixing the deeply broken farming model in Kenya. The case for putting more women in charge is powerfully illustrated by these examples.

Slowly, more women are making their way onto corporate boards, asking the tough questions and bringing new ideas into corporate life. Bill Johnson, former CEO of McDonald's Canada, said that having three women on the McDonald's Canada board changed things for the better for the restaurant chain. A 2006 study by Vicki Kramer, Alison Konrad and Sumru Erkut, published by the Wellesley Centers for Women, called three the magic number. It said that one woman, alone, struggles with being heard; two are stronger, better able to develop strategies for raising difficult issues; but three stops singling women out. It takes the focus off gender and shifts it onto what is being said. Three women appears to be the "critical mass" that makes their contribution less about representing "all women" and, instead, normalizes the fresh ideas and collaborative style that women can bring to the table. It's what helps men on boards say bye-bye to the female stereotype and hello to new ways of thinking and working.[71]

We would love to see more women on top, changing the world and all, but meanwhile our ambition for you is that you figure out what makes you happy and how to have that. If it's a corner office, we're in your corner. Women have so much to bring to leadership and every other step along the way to bigger jobs, but we have to bring it in our way, with openness, transparency, sharing, more equality, more diversity. It's okay to embrace your ambition of doing great things in the world whatever that means: local community efforts, politics, culture, business. No big title required. We celebrate you getting to your goals, whatever they are.

As millennials walk away from traditional goals and business models they deem to be too unforgiving, rigid and closed, we can model a different way. As twenty-something Nina B put it on the blog Techendo, "We should be seeking self-esteem, peace, confidence to take leaps of faith, and well-rounded happiness . . . We should be creating things, thinking of new ways to solve problems, starting our own businesses, taking breaks to go for walks with friends or feed our puppies. Do what helps you love yourself and helps you sleep at night."

These young women are looking to reinvent the world. If our

ambition went beyond status and money to include meaning and value, theirs goes even further. They're reaching all the way to sharing and happiness. And that's a very optimistic, exciting place for us to sign off.

Darlings, we hope a book written thanks to a bar of soap was well worth your precious free time. Put it in the bathroom and give a little light reading to the next woman with bigger life questions than the August 2010 *People* magazine can hope to answer. Then go out there and show them how it's done.

Acknowledgments

From the time our editor at HarperCollins, Kate Cassaday, first introduced herself after the keynote speech we gave at Toronto's Women of Influence event, saying, "Your story is a book" with a 100-watt smile, it would be over five years before that book would be born. The ten pages of speaking notes we used to tell our unusual career story at the annual businesswomen's lunch didn't seamlessly spool out into over 250 book pages, to understate.

We thank Kate for so many things. First, for getting us into a boardroom at HarperCollins to hear a chorus of "We'd love to publish your story," and soon after, for buying in to our pitch for a book, with a whole choir of voices, that would take exponentially more time and effort to deliver. She would insist that the project would still be waiting for us whenever we could return to it, after

Janet's husband was diagnosed with colon cancer. Even as many months went by and we expected the project to inevitably fold, Kate not only stood by her words, she delivered warm cookies and a steady stream of support and encouragement as Janet endured the crisis of a lifetime. Kate was the fearless leader of *Darling, You Can't Do Both*, with incredible skill as an editor and unwavering focus on the big picture.

Massive thanks go to Eleanor Beaton. Without her shaping, editing, research and enthusiasm, it may have taken another five years to complete this book. Siri Agrell was pivotal to getting lift-off, helping us wrestle the structure of the book to the ground with a toddler at her ankles and a new baby on one hip.

We're indebted to the many wonderful women and men who talked with us and agreed to let us share their experiences and wisdom. We've learned very much in the process, and made some new friends, too. We're so grateful to Sarah Scott and Amy Cross, who reached out to their big networks to add to the tapestry. And to Lily Kim for many hours of research.

Ogilvy & Mather gave us an environment where we could grow and thrive for over twenty years. Dozens of exceptional humans in the network mentored and taught us, including our employees. Big love to the miraculous Marina Pietracci, who looked after us, ran interference and was our third head for so long. Special thanks to Mark Hilltout, Steve Landsberg and Rick Boyko, who handed us the keys and watched us drive.

Thank you to Lily Vonk, who was a tween at the outset of book writing and is now a young woman. She was a constant thread of youthful perspective with ideas, disagreements, keen observations and endless patience for the project that, ironically, meant her mom was spread even thinner.

Mille grazie to Devin Monajem, all grown up from the boy who thought women ran the world, into the young man of the future: funny, wise, intuitive, clever and kind. His research chops were invaluable. His kitchen skills too, as he cooked many a Sunday dinner when his mom had no time.

To the loved ones who provided ideas, references, inspiration and endless encouragement, you made all the difference (especially through the tough stretches that life threw at us): dear fathers, Morris Kestin and Paul Miller; Steve Mykolyn; Jean Taylor; John, Doug and Leigh Miller; Leslie, Paulee, Philip and Maryse Kestin; Fetneh Monajem; Joyce Vanaman. And thank you to the friends who contributed stories, played sounding boards, and were still our friends even though we had to beg off doing the "'fun stuff" more often than we can count: Daryl Aitken, Anne Sutherland, Judith Wright and Diana Gibbs.

And finally to Mick Ebeling, who yelled, "Just do it!" through the car phone when it was exactly what we needed to hear.

Notes

1   Youngjoo Cha and Kim A. Weeden, "Overwork and the Slow Convergence in the Gender Gap in Wages," *Gender & Society*, January 24, 2013, doi: 101177/0891243212470510.

2   Sarah B. Weir, "American Women Crushed for Time: Have Themselves to Blame?" Yahoo Shine, March 7, 2012, www.shine.yahoo.com.

3   Gloria Galloway and Josh Lingrove, "Canadians' Leisure Time Shrinking," *The Globe and Mail*, June 15, 2010 (http://www.theglobeandmail.com/news/national/canadians-leisure-time-shrinking/article4389644/).

4   Anne Kingston, "Richer, Happier, Fitter? Not for Female Executives," *Macleans*, November 12, 2012 (http://www2.macleans.ca/2012/11/12/the-wealth-health-paradox/).

5   Centers for Disease Control and Prevention, "Women's Safety and Health Issues at Work," last updated July 10, 2013, http://www.cdc.gov/niosh/topics/women/work-structure.html.

6   Tim Kreider, "The 'Busy' Trap," *The New York Times*, June 30, 2012 (http://opinionator.blogs.nytimes.com/2012/06/30/the-busy-trap/?_php=true&_type=blogs&_r=0).

7   Alice H. Eagly and Linda L. Carli, *Through the Labyrinth: The Truth about How Women Become Leaders* (Boston: Harvard Business Press, 2007), page no. 55.

8   Tracy McVeigh, "Forty Years of Feminism—but Women Still Do Most of the Housework," *The Observer*, March 10, 2012.

9   Michelle Castillo, "Doing Household Chores May Mean Less Sex for Married Men," CBS News, January 31, 2013.

10   Pew Research Center, "Modern Parenthood: Roles of Moms and Dads Converge as They Balance Work and Family," March 13, 2013, http://www.pewsocialtrends.org/files/2013/03/FINAL_modern_parenthood_03-2013.pdf.

11   Brad Harrington, Fred Van Deusen, Jennifer Sabatini Fraone, *The New Dad: A Work (and Life) in Process* (Boston College Center for Work & Family, 2010), http://www.bc.edu/content/dam/files/centers/cwf/pdf/The%20New%20Dad%20 2013%20FINAL.pdf.

12   Stephen Benard, In Paik, and Shelley J. Correll, "Cognitive Bias and the Motherhood Penalty," *Hastings Law Journal* 59 (2008): 101–29.

13   Leah Goldman, "It's Called Compromise," *Harvard Political Review*, July 4, 2012 (http://harvardpolitics.com/united-states/its-called-compromise/).

14   Herminia Ibarra, Robin Ely, and Deborah Kolb, "Women Rising: The Unseen Barriers," *Harvard Business Review*, September 2013 (http://hbr.org/2013/09/women-rising-the-unseen-barriers/).

15   Ibid.

16   Anne Kingston, "Why Women Can't Get Ahead," *The Globe and Mail*, November 21, 2005 (http://www.theglobeandmail.com/report-on-business/why-women-cant-get-ahead/article1130890/?page=all).

17   U.S. President Barack Obama's speech in honor of National Mentoring Month, January 20, 2010.

18   Diana Bilimoria and Sandy Kristin Piderit, eds., *The Handbook on Women in Business and Management* (Cheltenham: Edward Elgar Publishing Limited, 2007), page no. 159.

19   Zvika Krieger, "So What if Tech Start-Ups Are Small? Their Job-Creation Impact Is Big," *The Atlantic*, October 8, 2012 (http://www.theatlantic.com/business/archive/2012/10/so-what-if-tech-start-ups-are-small-their-job-creation-impact-is-big/263332/).

20   Heather Boushey and Sarah Jane Glynn, "There Are Significant Business Costs to Replacing Employees," Center for American Progress, November 16, 2012 (http://www.americanprogress.org/wp-content/uploads/2012/11/CostofTurnover.pdf).

21   Knowledge@Wharton, "Do Women Shy Away from Promotions?" (http://knowledge.wharton.upenn.edu/article/do-women-shy-away-from-promotions/).

22   Andrew McMains, "Why the Average Barista Gets More Training than Most Agency Staffers," *Adweek*, March 21, 2011 (http://www.adweek.com/news/advertising-branding/why-average-barista-gets-more-training-most-agency-staffers-126034).

23   Ray Williams, "Like It or Not, Millennials Will Change the Workplace," *Financial Post*, September 16, 2013 (http://business.financialpost.com/2013/09/16/like-it-or-not-millennials-will-change-the-workplace/).

24   Graduate School of Arts and Sciences Teaching Center, Columbia University, "Gender Issues in the College Classroom" (http://www.columbia.edu/cu/tat/pdfs/gender.pdf).

25   Allyson Zimmermann, "Sponsorship: It's Not Who You Know but Who Knows You," *The Guardian*, July 8, 2013 (http://www.theguardian.com/women-in-leadership/2013/jul/08/sponsorship-who-knows-you).

26   Catalyst, "Sponsorship/Mentoring" (http://www.catalyst.org/knowledge/topics/ sponsorshipmentoring).

27   Joann S. Lublin, "When Women Mentor Too Much," *The Wall Street Journal*, October 11, 2013 (http://online.wsj.com/news/articles/SB1000142405270230338 2004579129273775055280).

28   Ibid.

29   Karen Phillips, "The Lessons I've Learned From My Nine-Year Mentoring Relationship," *The Guardian*, September 9, 2013.

30   The Ninety-Nines, Inc. (http://www.ninety-nines.org/index.cfm/advancing_ women_pilots.htm).

31   Emily Wall, "Mentoring the Mentor," *49 Writers* (blog), April 3, 2013, (http://49writers.blogspot.ca/2013/04/emily-wall-mentoring-mentor.html).

32   Catalyst, "The Double-Bind Dilemma for Women in Leadership: Damned if You Do, Doomed if You Don't," July 2007 (http://www.catalyst.org/knowledge/ double-bind-dilemma-women-leadership-damned-if-you-do-doomed-if-you- dont-0).

33   Victoria L. Brescoll and Eric Luis Uhlmann, "Can an Angry Woman Get Ahead?: Status Conferral, Gender and Expression of Emotion in the Workplace," *Psychological Science* 19 (March 2008): 268–275.

34   Daniel Bates, "Women Who Want to Succeed at Work Should Shut Up—While Men Who Want the Same Should Keep Talking," *Daily Mail*, May 17, 2012 (http://www.dailymail.co.uk/news/article-2146015/Women-want-succeed-work- shut--men-want-talking.html).

35   Ibid.

36   *How Smart Can We Get?* directed by Terri Randall (NOVA scienceNOW, aired October 24, 2012, on PBS).

37   Meghan Casserly, "The Real Origins of the Gender Pay Gap—and How We Can Turn It Around," *Forbes*, May 7, 2012 (http://www.forbes.com/sites/meghancas- serly/2012/07/05/real-origins-gender-pay-gap-how-we-can-turn-it-around/).

38 Borgna Brunner, "The Equal Pay Act: A History of Pay Inequity in the U.S.," Infoplease (http://www.infoplease.com/spot/equalpayact1.html).

39 Joseph Stromberg, "Are Scientists Sexist? New Study Identifies a Gender Bias," Smithsonian.com, Sept 24, 2012 (http://www.smithsonianmag.com/science-nature/are-scientists-sexist-new-study-identifies-a-gender-bias-47610982/).

40 Joyce Routsen, "Networking Is More than Lots of Names Says Heidi Roizen," Stanford Graduate School of Business, November 1, 2009 (http://www.gsb.stanford.edu/news/headlines/heidiroizen.html).

41 Catalyst, "High-Potential Employees in the Pipeline: Maximizing the Talent Pool in Canadian Organizations," December 2013 (http://www.catalyst.org/knowledge/high-potential-employees-pipeline-maximizing-talent-pool-canadian-organizations).

42 Lydia Dishman, "The One Career Mistake That'll Set You Back $500,000," *Fast Company*, 2012 (http://www.fastcompany.com/3003018/one-career-mistake-that-ll-set-you-back-500000).

43 Victoria Pynchon, "Woman Physician, Negotiate Thyself or Lose $350,000," *Forbes*, June 13, 2012.

44 U.S. Census, 2011.

45 Reshma Jagsi, Kent A. Griffith, Abigail Stewart, Dana Sambuco, Rochelle DeCastro, and Peter A. Ubel, "Gender Differences in the Salaries of Physician Researchers," *The Journal of the American Medical Association* 307, no. 22 (June 13, 2012): 2410–2417.

46 Report Shows Pay Gaps Widening Among Partners, AmLaw Daily, September 19, 2012; via adamsmithesq.com.

47 Carol Hymowitz, "Women Put Nose to the Grindstone, and Miss Opportunities," *The Wall Street Journal*, February 3, 2004.

48 Allianz, "Women, Money and Power," The 2013 Allianz Women, Money, and Power Study, https://www.allianzlife.com/retirement/retirement_insights/women_money_power.aspx.

49   Tara Siegel Bernard, "A Toolkit for Women Seeking a Raise," *The New York Times*, May 14, 2010.

50   Christina Boufis, "A Case for Salary Transparency," Little Pink Book, May 20, 2012.

51   Daniel G. O'Leary, "Women in Leadership Positions—Must They Work Harder? Yes" (http://www.insidebusiness360.com/index.php/women-in-leadership-positions-must-they-work-harder-yes-21930/).

52   Marianne Bertrand, Claudia Goldin, and Lawrence F. Katz, "Dynamics of the Gender Gap for Young Professionals in the Corporate and Financial Sectors," *American Economic Journal: Applied Economics* 2, no. 3 (July 2010): 228–255.

53   Joanna Barsh, Sandrine Devillard, and Jin Wang, "The Global Gender Agenda," McKinsey Quarterly, November 2012, http://www.mckinsey.com/insights/organization/the_global_gender_agenda.

54   Hannah Seligson, "Nurturing a Baby and a Start-Up Business," *The New York Times*, June 9, 2012 (http://www.nytimes.com/2012/06/10/business/nurturing-a-baby-and-a-start-up-business.html?pagewanted=all).

55   Ana Dutra, "Motherhood and Leadership Agility," *Forbes*, May 2011 (http://www.forbes.com/sites/anadutra/2011/05/09/motherhood-and-leadership-agility).

56   Amanda Robb, "Stella & Dot's CEO on the Brink of Making a Billion," *More* (http://www.more.com/dot-jewelry-ceo-jessica-herrin).

57   Hannah Seligson, "When the Work-Life Scales Are Unequal," *The New York Times*, September 1, 2012 (http://www.nytimes.com/2012/09/02/business/straightening-out-the-work-life-balance.html?pagewanted=all).

58   Credit Suisse Research Institute, "Gender Diversity and Corporate Performance," August 2012 (https://www.credit-suisse.com/newsletter/doc/gender_diversity.pdf).

59   Lynette Allen, "Women Don't Network—It Seems We Just Don't Get It!", http://herinvitation-test.com/blog/women-don%E2%80%99t-network-%E2%80%93-it-seems-we-just-don%E2%80%99t-get-it?page=2

60   Tahl Raz, "The 10 Secrets of a Master Networker," *Inc.*, January 1, 2003 (http://www.inc.com/magazine/20030101/25049.html).

61   Frieda Klotz, "How Your Gender Affects Your Networking Skills," *Forbes*, November 18, 2011 (http://www.forbes.com/sites/friedaklotz/2011/11/18/how-gender-affects-your-business-networking/).

62   Meghan Casserly, "U.S. Tops List of Best Countries for Women Entrepreneurs," *Forbes*, April 6, 2013 (http://www.forbes.com/sites/meghancasserly/2013/06/04/america-tops-dell-list-of-best-countries-for-women-entrepreneurs/).

63   Tom Post, "Around the World, Women Entrepreneurs Are on the Rise," *Forbes*, March 27, 2013 (http://www.forbes.com/sites/tompost/2013/03/27/around-the-world-women-entrepreneurs-are-on-the-rise/); Rebekah Epstein, "Leadership Lessons from Young Female Entrepreneurs," *Entrepreneur*, December 17, 2013 (http://www.entrepreneur.com/article/230409/).

64   Joanna Barsh and Lareina Yee, "Unlocking the Full Potential of Women at Work," McKinsey & Company, April 2011 (http://online.wsj.com/public/resources/documents/womenreportnew.pdf).

65   Women in Power Discussion Forum, *The Globe and Mail*, October 8, 2010.

66   David Thomas, "Me and My Brand: Sharon MacLeod and Unilever," *Marketing*, November 27, 2013.

67   L. Frank Baum, *The Wonderful Wizard of Oz* (New York: Knopf, 1900).

68   Melanie Kirkpatrick, "Having It All, Including Doubt," *The Wall Street Journal*, November 9, 2011 (http://online.wsj.com/news/articles/SB10001424052970204528204577008973326339502).

69   Richard Blackwell, "Most Executives Not Concerned by Number of Women in the Boardroom," *The Globe and Mail*, December 16, 2013 (http://www.theglobeandmail.com/report-on-business/most-executives-not-concerned-by-number-of-women-in-c-suite/article15978321/).

70   Based on the research of David Matsa and Amalia Miller, "Is There a Female Leadership Style?" *Kellogg Insight*, September 2013 (http://insight.kellogg.northwestern.edu/article/is_there_a_female_leadership_style/).

71   Vicki W. Kramer, Alison M. Konrad, and Sumru Erkut, "Critical Mass on Corporate Boards: Why Three or More Women Enhance Governance," Wellesley, MA: Wellesley Centers for Women, 2006   (http://www.wcwonline.org/pdf/Critical-MassExecSummary.pdf).